AF598714

TRADIVOX

VOLUME XV

TRADIVOX

CATHOLIC CATECHISM INDEX

VOLUME XV

Quebec

Edited by
Aaron Seng

SOPHIA INSTITUTE PRESS
MANCHESTER, NEW HAMPSHIRE

South Bend, Indiana
www.Tradivox.com

This book is an original derivative work comprised of newly typeset and reformatted editions of the following Catholic catechisms, once issued with ecclesiastical approval and now found in the public domain:

Denaut, Pierre. *An Abridgment of Christian Doctrine*. Montreal: J. Brown, 1812.

Signay, Joseph. *An Abridgment of the Quebec Catechism*.
Quebec: J. B. Fréchette & Co., 1834.

Bishops of Canada. *The Catechism of the Ecclesiastical Provinces of Quebec, Montreal, Ottawa*. Quebec: A. Coté & Co., 1888.

Scripture references follow the Douay-Rheims Bible,
per the imprint of John Murphy Company (Baltimore, 1899).

Cover and interior design by Perceptions Design Studio.

Sophia Institute Press
Box 5284, Manchester, NH 03108
1-800-888-9344

www.SophiaInstitute.com

ISBN 978-1-64413-378-1
LCCN 2023932704

Dedicated with love and deepest respect
to all the English Martyrs and Confessors.
Orate pro nobis.

CONTENTS

ACKNOWLEDGMENTS

THE publication of this series is due primarily to the generosity of countless volunteers and donors from several countries. Special thanks are owed to Mr. and Mrs. Phil Seng, Mr. and Mrs. Michael Over, Mr. and Mrs. Jim McElwee, Mr. and Mrs. John Brouillette, Mr. and Mrs. Thomas Scheibelhut, Mr. and Mrs. Kyle Barriger, as well the visionary priests and faithful of St. Stanislaus Bishop and Martyr parish in South Bend, Indiana, and St. Patrick's Oratory in Green Bay, Wisconsin. May God richly reward their commitment to handing on the Catholic faith.

FOREWORD

The Catholic faith remains always the same throughout the centuries and millennia until the coming of our Lord at the end of the time, likewise "Jesus Christ is the same yesterday, today and forever" (Heb 13:8). The Catholic faith is "the faith, which was once delivered unto the saints" (Jude 1:3). The Magisterium of the Church teaches us solemnly the same truth in the following words of the First Vatican Council: "The doctrine of the faith which God has revealed, is put forward not as some philosophical discovery capable of being perfected by human intelligence, but as a divine deposit committed to the spouse of Christ to be faithfully protected and infallibly promulgated. Hence, too, that meaning of the sacred dogmas is ever to be maintained, which has once been declared by holy mother Church, and there must never be any abandonment of this sense under the pretext or in the name of a more profound understanding. May understanding, knowledge and wisdom increase as ages and centuries roll along, and greatly and vigorously flourish, in each and all, in the individual and the whole Church: but this only in its own proper kind, that is to say, in the same doctrine, the same sense, and the same understanding (cf. Vincentius Lerinensis, *Commonitorium*, 28)."[1]

An authentically Catholic catechism has the function of learning and teaching the unchanging Catholic faith throughout all generations. The Roman Pontiffs indeed, taught: "There is nothing more effective than catechetical instruction to spread the glory of God and to secure the salvation of souls."[2] Saint Pius X said, that "the great loss of souls is due to ignorance

[1] Vatican I, Dogmatic Constitution *Dei Filius de fide catholica*, Ch. 4

[2] Pope Benedict XIV, Apostolic Constitution *Etsi minime*, n. 13

of divine things."[3] Therefore, the traditional catechisms have enduring value in our own day and age, which is marked by an enormous doctrinal confusion, which reigns in the life of the Church in the past six decades, and which reaches its peak in our days.

I welcome and bless the great project of the "Tradivox" in cataloguing and preserving the hundreds of long-lost Catholic catechisms issued with episcopal approval over the last millennium. This project will convincingly show the essentially unchanging nature of the apostolic doctrine across time and space, and so I invite the faithful of the entire world to support this historic effort, as we seek to restore the perennial catechism of the Church. The project of a catechism restoration on behalf of "Tradivox" will surely be of great benefit not only to many confused and disoriented Catholic faithful, but also to all people who are sincerely seeking the ultimate and authentic truth about God and man, which one can find only in the Catholic and apostolic faith, and which is the only religion and faith willed by God and to which God calls all men.

+Athanasius Schneider, O.R.C.,
Titular Bishop of Celerina
Auxiliary Bishop of the Archdiocese of Saint Mary in Astana

[3] Cf. Pope St. Pius X, Encyclical *Acerbo nimis*, n. 27

SERIES EDITOR'S

PREFACE

SOME are surprised to find that when a given Catholic is asked to "look something up in the catechism," he may well respond: "Which one?" The history of the Catholic Church across the last millennium is in fact filled with the publication of numerous catechisms, issued in every major language on earth; and for centuries, these concise "guidebooks" to Catholic doctrine have served countless men and women seeking a clear and concise presentation of that faith forever entrusted by Jesus Christ to his one, holy, Catholic, and apostolic Church.

Taken together, the many catechisms issued with episcopal approval can offer a kind of "window" on to the universal ordinary magisterium—a glimpse of those truths which have been held and taught in the Church *everywhere, always, and by all.* For, as St. Paul reminds us, the tenets of this Faith do not change from age to age: "Jesus Christ yesterday and today and the same for ever. Be not led away with various and strange doctrines" (Heb 13:8-9).

The catechisms included in our *Tradivox Catholic Catechism Index* are selected for their orthodoxy and historical significance, in the interest of demonstrating to contemporary readers the remarkable continuity of Catholic doctrine across time and space. Long regarded as reliable summaries of Church teaching on matters of faith and morals, we are proud to reproduce these works of centuries past, composed and endorsed by countless priests, bishops, and popes devoted to "giving voice to tradition."

In This Volume

In the long history of the catechetical genre, texts originating from the New World occupy an understandably recent portion of the timeline. In this volume, we turn for the first time to the North American continent, reclaiming three successive forms of what came to be known as the "Quebec Catechism"—the most widely used official catechism in the Canadian provinces for nearly three centuries.

The early evangelization of the Americas began in the same century as the Protestant Revolt, the Council of Trent, and major advances in mechanical printing, and it was not long before catechisms began to appear across the oceans. In addition to bringing European catechisms from overseas, members of the various Catholic missionary orders were dedicated to producing instructive works that were adapted to the new circumstances of the foreign missions. Missionary priests especially worked tirelessly, and often in concert with native speakers, to produce multi-language catechisms that could be employed within the far-flung territories in which the gospel was taking root. Considering the many challenges involved, they appeared with amazing rapidity; and in some cases, these books were the first ever printed in their respective languages—if not the first to be printed on the entire continent. Latin, vernacular, bilingual, and even trilingual catechisms were composed for Mexico (1539), India (1546), Japan (1570), Peru (1584), China (1584), Vietnam (1629), and Huronia (1632), to name a few. The latter deserves special mention here, as it was the work of the great Jesuit missionary priest St. Jean de Brebeuf (1593–1649) and forms the historical backdrop for the Canadian catechisms that are contained in this volume.

Brebeuf's catechism was a translation of Fr. Ledesma's *The Christian Doctrine*,[1] and holds the dual honor of being the first book ever composed in the Wendat language as well as the first written attempt to make Christianity intelligible to the pagans of North America. Apart from the innate complexities of the tribal tongues (a demonstration of which may be observed in the

[1] Ledesma's catechism may be found in Volume I of this series.

fact that one of these—the Navajo language—was employed by the Allies as an unbreakable military code during World War II), how could sin, grace, or salvation be discussed with peoples lacking any terms for guilt or innocence, or any notion of the soul? How could the mystery of the Eucharist be rightly communicated to people practicing ritual cannibalism? As Brebeuf himself wrote to his superiors in France:

> Every day we discover new secrets in this science, which for the present hinders us from sending anything to be printed. We know now, thank God, sufficient to understand and to be understood, but not yet to publish. It is indeed an exceedingly laborious task to endeavor to understand in all points a foreign tongue, very abundant, and as different from our European languages as heaven is from earth—and that without master or books. ... We all work at it diligently; it is one of our most common occupations.[2]

Despite such immense linguistic challenges, the evangelization of Canada owes a great deal to the efforts of the heroic martyr St. Jean de Brebeuf, who went on to publish both a Wendat catechism and dictionary that would prove instrumental for the early catechetical efforts in New France.

As years went by, the majority of Catholic settlers in early Canada would come from France or places of French extraction, leading to the promulgation of what appears to be the first regional catechism issued by episcopal authority in the area: *Catéchisme du diocèse de Québec*, which was printed in Paris in 1702 and shipped to the continent. Adaptations, derivations, and entirely separate works continued to appear there and in other dioceses (e.g., the respected *Catéchisme du diocèse de Sens*, 1739), but the proven structure and widespread use of the original "Quebec Catechism" saw it continuously adapted and reprinted through two generations, eventually being printed on the continent itself in 1782. By this time, copiously detailed linguistic records and dictionaries of the newfound languages in North America and other mission territories had been composed, allowing catechesis among the tribal peoples to proceed with much greater effect. As

[2] Reuben G. Thwaites, ed., *The Jesuit Relations and Allied Documents*, vol. 10 (Cleveland: The Burrows Brothers Company, 1897), 55.

seen with the work of St. Jean de Brebeuf, this progress was due in great measure to the work of the early Jesuits and their successors; in fact, prior to their suppression in 1773, the Jesuit order alone may be credited with having composed over 160 catechisms, and in no fewer than 124 languages and 6 different dialects around the world. Such a degree of staggering editorial work inspired still further translations of catechisms that had already stood the test of time in many places; works like the well-known "Douay Catechism,"[3] adapted in Canada toward the end of the 18th century for use by "such of this diocese as have no other means of instruction but in the English tongue." The present volume recovers the 1812 Montreal edition of this work without any change, excepting the addition of a few subheadings to render the arrangement of the text a bit clearer.

English translations of the Quebec Catechism did not appear until considerably later, as the famous catechism of Bishop James Butler[4] was already in widespread use among English-speaking Catholics throughout North America; a fact well evidenced by the decision of the First Provincial Council of Quebec in 1851, which ordered only two catechisms for use in the country: Butler's Catechism for English-speakers, and the Quebec Catechism for those speaking French. By then, a number of English abridgments had already made it into circulation, and as the number of native English-speakers among the North American hierarchy increased through the mid-1800s, so did the number of Canadian catechisms in that tongue. The present volume recovers the 1834 edition of *An Abridgment of the Quebec Catechism*, "revised and authorized by His Lordship, the Right Reverend Joseph Signay, Bishop of Quebec." Although we have retained the entirety of the original base text, we have taken the liberty of expanding a number of abbreviations that were necessitated by page constraints in the original, such as the holy names of Jesus and Mary, which are here rendered in their entirety. We have also specified several chapter subheadings, again in the interest of rendering the inherent arrangement of the text more evident to the reader.

[3] The 1649 original is found in Volume II of this series.

[4] Found in Volume IV of this series.

In 1888, in order to promote greater ecclesiastical unity among the diverse Canadian dioceses and to supply for an evident lack of uniformity in catechetical texts (a major concern of the Plenary Synods of Baltimore to the south), the bishops of Quebec, Montreal, and Ottawa jointly issued what would become the most enduring and recognizable Canadian catechism: *The Catechism of the Ecclesiastical Provinces of Quebec, Montreal, Ottawa*. This text would remain the dominant catechism in Canada until the latter half of the 20th century, generally under the persistent moniker of the "Quebec Catechism." In our own time, like the Maynooth Catechism in Ireland or the Baltimore Catechism in the United States, the very mention of the Quebec Catechism is still able to conjure memories of chalk dust and schoolyards for Catholics in Canada. Apart from the addition of a few clarifying subheadings, the 1888 original has been retained here without alteration, including the asterisks used to designate the most basic material.

Editorial Note

Our *Catholic Catechism Index* series generally retains only the doctrinal content of those catechisms it seeks to reproduce, as well as that front matter most essential to establishing the credibility of each work as an authentic expression of the Church's common doctrine, e.g., any episcopal endorsement, *nihil obstat*, or *imprimatur*. However, it should be noted that especially prior to the eighteenth century, a number of catechisms were so immediately and universally received as reliably orthodox texts (often simply by the reputation of the author or publisher), that they received no such "official" approval; or if they did, it was often years later and in subsequent editions. We therefore include both the original printing date in our Table of Contents, and further edition information in the Preface above.

Our primary goal has been to bring these historical texts back into publication in readable English copy. Due to the wide range of time periods, cultures, and unique author styles represented in this series, we have made a number of editorial adjustments to allow for a less fatiguing read, more rapid cross-reference throughout the series, and greater research potential for the future. While not affecting the original content, these adjustments

Woodcut depicting an early method used in the production of Catholic catechisms, circa 1568.

have included adopting a cleaner typesetting and simpler standard for capitalization and annotation, as well as remedying certain anachronisms in spelling or grammar.

At the same time, in deepest respect for the venerable age and subject matter of these works, we have been at pains to adhere as closely as possible to the original text: retaining archaisms such as "doth" and "hallowed," and avoiding any alterations that might affect the doctrinal content or authorial voice. We have painstakingly restored original artwork wherever possible, and where the rare explanatory note has been deemed necessary, it is not made in the text itself, but only in a marginal note. In some cases, our editorial refusal to "modernize" the content of these classical works may require a higher degree of attention from today's reader, who we trust will be richly rewarded by the effort.

We pray that our work continues to yield highly readable, faithful reproductions of these time-honored monuments to Catholic religious instruction: catechisms once penned, promulgated, and praised by bishops across the globe. May these texts that once served to guide and shape the faith and lives of millions now do so again; and may the scholars and saints once involved in their first publication now intercede for all who take them up anew. *Tolle lege!*

Sincerely in Christ,
Aaron Seng

TRADIVOX

VOLUME XV

AN

ABRIDGMENT

OF

CHRISTIAN DOCTRINE.

PUBLISHED FOR THE USE OF THE

DIOCESE OF QUEBEC.

MONTREAL:

Printed and Sold by J. Brown, Stationer,
opposite the Seminary.

1812.

Original Title Page

AN

ABRIDGMENT

OF

CHRISTIAN DOCTRINE.

PUBLISHED FOR THE USE OF THE

DIOCESE OF QUEBEC.

MONTREAL:

**Printed and Sold by J. Brown, Stationer,
opposite the Seminary.**

1812.

QUEBEC, 25th October, 1800.

We the undersigned do permit the use of this *Abridgment of Christian Doctrine*, to such of this diocese as have no other means of instruction but in the English tongue.

J. O. PLESSIS,
Vic. Gén.

An Abridgment of Christian Doctrine

God and Faith in General

1. **Who made you?**
God.

2. **Why did he make you?**
That I might know him, love him, and serve him in this world, and be happy with him forever in the next.

3. **To whose likeness did he make you?**
To his own image and likeness.

4. **Is this likeness in your body or in your soul?**
In my soul.

5. **In what is your soul like to God?**
Because my soul is a spirit endowed with understanding and free will, and is immortal, that is to say, it can never die.

6. **In what else?**
That as in God there is one God and three Persons, so in man there is one soul and three powers.

7. **Which are the three powers?**
Will, memory, and understanding.

8. **Which must we take most care of: our body or our soul?**
Of our soul.

9. **Why so?**
Because: "What will it avail a man to gain the whole world, and lose his own soul?"[1]

10. **What must we do to save our soul?**
We must worship God by faith, hope, and charity: that is, we must believe in him, hope in him, and love him, with all our hearts.

11. **What is faith?**
It is to believe without doubting all that God teaches; because he is the very truth, and cannot deceive, nor be deceived.

12. **And how shall we know what the things are which God teaches?**
From the testimony of the Catholic Church of God, which he has established by innumerable miracles, and illustrated by the lives and deaths of innumerable saints.

The Apostles' Creed

13. **What are the chief things which God teaches?**
They are contained in the Apostles' Creed.

[1] Mt 16:26

14. **Say the Apostles' Creed.**
I believe in God the Father Almighty, Creator of heaven and earth, and in Jesus Christ his only Son our Lord, who was conceived by the Holy Ghost; born of the Virgin Mary; suffered under Pontius Pilate, was crucified, dead, and buried; he descended into hell; the third day he rose again from the dead; he ascended into heaven; sits at the right hand of God the Father Almighty; from thence he shall come to judge the living and the dead. I believe in the Holy Ghost, the holy Catholic Church, the communion of saints, the forgiveness of sins, the resurrection of the body, and life everlasting. Amen.

THE FIRST ARTICLE OF THE CREED

15. **Which is the first article of the Apostles' Creed?**
I believe in God the Father Almighty, Creator of heaven and earth.

16. **What is God?**
God is a Spirit, the Creator and sovereign Lord of all things.

17. **Why is he called, "Almighty"?**
Because he can do all things whatever he pleases, and nothing is hard or impossible to him.

18. **Why is he called, "Creator of heaven and earth"?**
Because he made heaven and earth, and all things out of nothing, by his only Word.

19. **Had God any beginning?**
No; he always was, is, and always will be.

20. **Where is God?**
God is everywhere.

21. **Does God know and see all things?**
Yes, he does know and see all things.

22. **Has God any body?**
No, God has no body; he is a pure Spirit.

23. **How many gods are there?**
There is but one God.

24. **Are there more Persons than one in God?**
Yes; in God there are three Persons.

25. **Which are they?**
God the Father, God the Son, and God the Holy Ghost.

26. **Are they not three gods?**
No; the Father, the Son, and the Holy Ghost, are all but one and the same God.

THE SECOND ARTICLE

27. **Which is the second article of the Creed?**
And in Jesus Christ his only Son our Lord.

28. **Who is Jesus Christ?**
He is the only Son of God the Father, the second Person of the Blessed Trinity, true God and true man.

29. **Why is he true God?**
Because he has the nature of God, being of the selfsame substance with God the Father.

30. **Why is he true man?**
Because he has also the nature of man, being the Son of the Blessed Virgin, and has a body and soul like unto us.

31. **Was Jesus Christ always God?**
Yes, he was always God, equal to his Father from all eternity.

32. **Was he always man?**
No, but only from the time of his incarnation.

33. **How many natures are there in Jesus Christ?**
Two; the nature of God, and the nature of man.

34. **How many Persons are there in Jesus Christ?**
Only one; which is the Person of God the Son.

35. **Why was he made man?**
To save us from sin and hell.

THE THIRD ARTICLE

36. **Which is the third article of the Creed?**
Who was conceived by the Holy Ghost, born of the Virgin Mary.

37. **How was Christ made man?**
He was conceived and made man by the power of the Holy Ghost, in the womb of the Virgin Mary, without having any man for his father.

38. **Where was our Savior born?**
In a stable in Bethlehem.

39. **Upon what day was he born?**
Upon Christmas day.

THE FOURTH ARTICLE

40. **Which is the fourth article of the Creed?**
Suffered under Pontius Pilate, was crucified, dead, and buried.

41. **What did Christ suffer?**
A bloody sweat, whipping at the pillar, crowning with thorns, and the carriage of his cross.

42. **What else?**
He was nailed to a cross, and died upon it between two thieves.

43. **Why did he suffer?**
For our sins.

44. **Upon what day did he suffer?**
On Good Friday.

45. **Where did he suffer?**
On Mount Calvary.

46. **Why do Catholics make the sign of the cross?**
To put us in mind of the Blessed Trinity, and that the second Person became man, and died on the cross.

47. **What puts us in mind of the Blessed Trinity when we make the sign of the cross?**
These words: "In the name of the Father, and of the Son, and of the Holy Ghost."

48. **What puts us in mind that Christ became man, and suffered on a cross?**
The very making or signing ourselves with the sign of the cross.

THE FIFTH ARTICLE

49. **Which is the fifth article of the Creed?**
He descended into hell; the third day he rose again from the dead.

50. **Whither did the soul of our Savior go after his death?**
His soul went down into that part of hell called limbo.

51. **What do you mean by *limbo*?**
I mean a place of rest, where the souls of the saints were.

52. **Did none go up to heaven before our Savior?**
No; they expected him to carry them up thither.

53. **What means: "The third day he rose again from the dead"?**
It means that, after he was dead and buried for part of three days, he raised himself to life again on the third day.

54. **On what day did Christ rise again from the dead?**
On Easter day.

THE SIXTH ARTICLE

55. **Which is the sixth article of the Creed?**
He ascended into heaven; sits at the right hand of God the Father Almighty.

56. **When did our Savior go up to heaven?**
Forty days after he rose again.

57. **Why is he said to sit at the right hand of God the Father? Has God the Father any hands?**
No; but the meaning of the word is that Christ, as man, occupies the next place to God in heaven, and as God, is equal to his Father in all things.

58. **On what day did our Savior go up to heaven?**
On Ascension day.

THE SEVENTH ARTICLE

59. **Which is the seventh article of the Creed?**
From thence he shall come to judge the living and the dead.

60. **Will Christ ever come again?**
Yes; he will come down from heaven at the last day to judge all men.

61. **What are the things he will judge?**
All our thoughts, words, and works.

62. **What will he say to the wicked?**
"Go, ye cursed, into everlasting fire."[2]

63. **What will he say to the just?**
"Come, ye blessed of my Father, receive ye the kingdom which is prepared for you."[3]

64. **Shall not every man be judged at his death as well as at the last day?**
Yes, he shall.

THE EIGHTH ARTICLE

65. **Which is the eighth article of the Creed?**
I believe in the Holy Ghost.

66. **Who is the Holy Ghost?**
He is the third Person of the Blessed Trinity.

[2] Mt 25:41
[3] Mt 25:34

67. **From whom doth he proceed?**
From the Father and the Son.

68. **Is he equal to them?**
Yes; he is the same Lord and God as they are.

69. **When did the Holy Ghost come down on the apostles in fiery tongues?**
On Whitsunday.

70. **Why did he come upon them?**
To enable them to preach the gospel, and to plant the Church.

THE NINTH ARTICLE

71. **Which is the ninth article of the Creed?**
I believe the holy Catholic Church; the communion of saints.

The Catholic Church

72. **What is the Catholic Church?**
All the faithful under one head.

73. **Who is that head?**
Christ Jesus our Lord.

74. **Has the Church any visible head on earth?**
Yes; the bishop of Rome, who is the successor of St. Peter, and commonly called "the pope."

75. **Why is he called "the pope"?**
Because the word *pope* signifies "father"; and the bishop of Rome, as head of the Church under Jesus Christ, is the common father of all the faithful.

76. **Has the Church of Christ any marks by which you may know it?**
Yes; it has these four marks: it is one, it is holy, it is catholic, and apostolical.

77. **How is the Church one?**
Because all its members agree in one faith, are all in one communion, and are all under one head.

78. **How is the Church holy?**
By teaching a holy doctrine, by inviting all to a holy life, and by the eminent holiness of so many thousands of her children.

79. **How is the Church catholic or universal?**
Because she subsists in all ages; teaches all nations; and maintains all truths.

80. **How is the Church apostolical?**
Because she comes down by a perpetual succession from the apostles of Christ, and has her doctrine, her orders, and her mission from them.

81. **Can the Church err in what she teaches?**
No; she cannot err in matters of faith.

82. **Why so?**
Because Christ has promised that hell's gates shall not prevail against his Church; and that the Holy Ghost shall teach her all truths; and that he himself will abide with her forever.

The Communion of Saints

83. **What is meant by "the communion of saints"?**
That in the Church of God there is a communion of all holy persons in all holy things.

84. **And have we any communion with the saints in heaven?**
Yes; we communicate with them, as our fellow members under the same head, Jesus Christ; and we are helped by their prayers.

85. **And are the souls in purgatory helped by our prayers?**
Yes, they are.

86. **What do you mean by *purgatory*?**
A middle state of souls, suffering for a time on account of their sins.

87. **In what cases do souls go to purgatory?**
When they die in lesser sins, which we call venial; or when they have not satisfied the justice of God for those mortal sins, of which they have repented and got pardon.

88. **How do you prove there is a purgatory?**
Because the scripture often teaches that God will render to every man according to his works, and that nothing defiled can enter heaven, and that some Christians shall be saved, "yet so as by fire."[4]

THE TENTH ARTICLE

89. **Which is the tenth article of the Creed?**
The forgiveness of sins.

90. **What is meant by this article?**
That there is in the Church of God a forgiveness of sins, for such as properly apply for it.

91. **To whom has Christ given power to forgive sins?**
To the apostles and their successors, the bishops and priests of the Church.

[4] 1 Cor 3:15

92. **By what sacraments are sins forgiven?**
By baptism and penance.

93. **What is sin?**
An offense of God, or any thought, word, or deed against the law of God.

94. **What is original sin?**
It is the sin in which we were born.

95. **How came we to be born in sin?**
By Adam's sin, when he ate the forbidden fruit.

96. **What is actual sin?**
All the sin we commit ourselves.

97. **What is mortal sin?**
That which kills the soul and deserves hell.

98. **How does mortal sin kill the soul?**
By destroying the life of the soul, which is the grace of God.

99. **What is venial sin?**
That which does not kill the soul yet displeases God.

THE ELEVENTH ARTICLE

100. **Which is the eleventh article of the Creed?**
The resurrection of the body.

101. **What means: "The resurrection of the body"?**
That we shall rise again with the same bodies at the day of judgment.

THE TWELFTH ARTICLE

102. **Which is the twelfth article of the Creed?**
Life everlasting.

103. **What means: "Life everlasting"?**
That the good shall live forever happy in heaven.

104. **What is the happiness of heaven?**
To see, love, and enjoy God forevermore.

105. **And shall not the wicked also live forever?**
They shall be punished forever in the flames of hell.

The Lord's Prayer and Hail Mary

106. **Will faith alone save us?**
No; it will not without good works.

107. **Can we do any good work toward our salvation of ourselves?**
No; we cannot without the help of God's grace.

108. **How may we obtain God's grace?**
By prayer and the holy sacraments.

109. **What is prayer?**
It is the raising up our mind to God.

110. **What think you of those who at their prayers think not of God nor of what they say?**
If these distractions are willful, such prayers, instead of pleasing God, offend him.

111. **Which is the best of all prayers?**
The Lord's Prayer.

112. **Who made the Lord's Prayer?**
Christ our Lord.

113. **Say the Lord's Prayer.**
Our Father who are in heaven, hallowed be thy name, thy kingdom come; thy will be done on earth as it is in heaven; give us this day our daily bread; and forgive us our trespasses as we forgive them that trespass against us; and lead us not into temptation, but deliver us from evil. Amen.

114. **Who is it that is here called, "Our Father"?**
God, who made us all, and who by his grace is the Father of all good Christians.

115. **Why do you say, "Our Father," and not, "My Father"?**
Because we are not to pray for ourselves alone, but for all others.

116. **What do we pray for when we say, "Hallowed be thy name"?**
That God may be honored and served by all his creatures.

117. **What means: "Thy kingdom come"?**
We pray that God may come, and be King in all our hearts by his grace; and bring us all hereafter to his heavenly kingdom.

118. **What means: "Thy will be done on earth as it is in heaven"?**
That God would enable us, by his grace, to do his will in all things as the blessed do in heaven.

119. **What means: "Give us this day our daily bread"?**
We beg by these words all necessaries for soul and body.

120. **What means: "Forgive us our trespasses as we forgive them that trespass against us"?**
We beg that God will forgive us our sins as we forgive others the injuries they do us.

121. **What means: "Lead us not into temptation"?**
That God would give us grace not to yield to temptation.

122. **What means: "Deliver us from evil"?**
We beg that God will free us from all evil of soul and body.

123. **May we desire the saints and angels to pray for us?**
Yes, we may.

124. **How do you prove that the saints and angels can hear us?**
"There shall be joy before the angels of God over one sinner that repents."[5]

125. **What is the prayer to our Blessed Lady, which the Church teaches us?**
The Hail Mary.

126. **Say the Hail Mary.**
Hail Mary, full of grace, our Lord is with thee; blessed art thou amongst women, and blessed is the fruit of thy womb, Jesus. Holy Mary, Mother of God, pray for us sinners, now and in the hour of our death. Amen.

127. **How many parts are there in the Hail Mary?**
Three parts.

[5] Lk 15:10

128. **Who made the two first parts?**
The angel Gabriel and St. Elizabeth, inspired by the Holy Ghost.

129. **Who made the third part?**
The Church of God; against those who denied the Virgin Mary to be the Mother of God.

130. **Why say you the Hail Mary so often?**
To put us in mind of the Son of God being made man for us.

131. **For what other reason?**
To honor the Blessed Virgin, Mother of God, and to beg her prayers for us.

The Ten Commandments

132. **How many commandments are there?**
Ten.

133. **Who gave the ten commandments?**
God himself in the old law, and Christ confirmed them in the new.

THE FIRST COMMANDMENT

134. **Which is the first commandment?**
"I am the Lord thy God who brought thee out of the land of Egypt, and out of the house of bondage. Thou shalt not have strange gods before me. Thou shalt not make to thyself any graven thing, nor the likeness of anything that is in heaven above, or in the earth beneath, or in the waters under the earth; thou shalt not adore them, or serve them."[6]

[6] Ex 20:2-5

135. **What are we commanded by this?**
To believe, hope, love, and serve one true and living God, and no more.

136. **What is forbidden by this commandment?**
To worship false gods or idols, or to give anything else whatsoever the honor which belongs to God.

137. **What else is forbidden by this commandment?**
All false religions and dealing with the devil; and enquiring after things to come, by fortune tellers, or superstitious practices.

138. **What else?**
All charms, spells, and heathenish observations of omens, dreams, and such like fooleries.

139. **Does this commandment forbid the making of images?**
It forbids the making of them so as to adore and serve them: that is, it forbids making them our gods.

140. **Does this commandment forbid all honor and veneration of the saints and angels?**
No; we are to honor them as God's special friends and servants, but not with the honor which belongs to God.

141. **And is it allowable to honor relics, crucifixes, and holy pictures?**
Yes; with an inferior and relative honor, as they relate to Christ and his saints and are memorials of them.

142. **May we not pray to relics or images?**
No, by no means; for they have no life or sense to help us.

THE SECOND COMMANDMENT

143. **What is the second commandment?**
"Thou shalt not take the name of the Lord thy God in vain."[7]

144. **What are we commanded by the second commandment?**
To speak with reverence of God and all holy things, and to keep our lawful oaths and vows.

145. **What are we forbid by it?**
All false, rash, unjust, and unnecessary oaths, as also cursing, blaspheming, and profane words.

THE THIRD COMMANDMENT

146. **What is the third commandment?**
"Remember that thou keep holy the sabbath day."[8]

147. **What are we commanded by this?**
To spend the Sunday in prayer and other religious duties.

148. **What do you mean by "religious duties"?**
Hearing Mass, going to the sacraments, and reading good books.

149. **What are we forbid by this commandment?**
All unnecessary work and sinful profanation of the Lord's day.

THE FOURTH COMMANDMENT

150. **What is the fourth commandment?**
"Honor thy father and thy mother."[9]

[7] Ex 20:7
[8] Ex 20:8
[9] Ex 20:12

151. **What are we commanded by the fourth commandment?**
To love, honor, and obey our parents in all that is not sin.

152. **Are we commanded to obey only our father and mother?**
Not only them, but also our bishops, pastors, magistrates, and masters.

153. **What is forbidden by this commandment?**
All contempt, stubbornness, and disobedience to our lawful superiors.

154. **And what is the duty of parents and other superiors?**
To take proper care of all under their charge; and to bring their children up in the fear of God.

THE FIFTH COMMANDMENT

155. **What is the fifth commandment?**
"Thou shalt not kill."[10]

156. **What are we forbidden by this commandment?**
All willful murder, hatred, and revenge.

157. **Does it forbid striking?**
Yes; as also anger, quarreling, and injurious words.

158. **What else?**
Giving scandal and bad example.

THE SIXTH COMMANDMENT

159. **What is the sixth commandment?**
"Thou shalt not commit adultery."[11]

[10] Ex 20:13
[11] Ex 20:14

160. **What is forbidden by this?**
All kind of sins of uncleanness with another's wife or husband.

161. **What else?**
All other kinds of immodesties, by kisses, touches, looks, words, or actions.

162. **And what ought we to think of immodest plays and comedies?**
That they are also forbidden by this commandment; and it is sinful to be present at them.

THE SEVENTH COMMANDMENT

163. **What is the seventh commandment?**
"Thou shalt not steal."[12]

164. **What is forbidden by this commandment?**
All unjust taking away, or keeping what belongs to others.

165. **What else?**
All manner of cheating in buying and selling; or any other way wronging our neighbor.

166. **Must we restore ill-gotten good?**
Yes, if we are able, or else the sin will not be forgiven; we must also pay our debts.

THE EIGHTH COMMANDMENT

167. **What is the eighth commandment?**
"Thou shalt not bear false witness against thy neighbor."[13]

[12] Ex 20:15
[13] Ex 20:16

168. **What is forbidden by this commandment?**
All false testimonies, rash judgments, and lies.

169. **What else?**
All backbiting and detraction, or any words or speeches by which our neighbor's honor or reputation is any ways hurt.

170. **What is he bound to do who has injured his neighbor by speaking ill of him?**
He must make him satisfaction, and restore his good name as far as he is able.

THE NINTH COMMANDMENT

171. **What is the ninth commandment?**
"Thou shalt not covet thy neighbor's wife."[14]

172. **What is forbidden by this?**
All lustful thoughts and desires, and all willful pleasure in the irregular motions of the flesh.

THE TENTH COMMANDMENT

173. **What is the tenth commandment?**
"Thou shalt not covet thy neighbor's goods."[15]

174. **What is forbidden by this?**
All covetous thoughts and unjust desires of our neighbor's goods and profits.

[14] Ex 20:17
[15] Ibid.

The Commandments of the Church

175. **Are we bound to obey the commandments of the Church?**
Yes, because Christ has said to the pastors of the Church: "He that heareth you, heareth me; and he that despiseth you, despiseth me."[16]

176. **How many are the commandments of the Church?**
Chiefly six.

177. **Which are they?**
1. To keep certain appointed days holy; with obligation of hearing Mass, and resting from servile works.
2. To fast Lent, vigils commanded by the Church, and Ember days; also to abstain from flesh on the three Rogation days, St. Mark, the Sundays of Lent, and all Fridays and Saturdays—Saturdays between Christmas day and Candlemas excepted.
3. To confess our sins to our pastor, at least once a year.
4. To receive the Blessed Sacrament once a year, and that at Easter, or thereabout.
5. To pay tithes to our pastor.
6. Not to solemnize marriage at certain times, nor within certain degrees of kindred, nor privately without witnesses.

178. **Why does the Church command us to fast?**
That by fasting we may satisfy God for our sins.

179. **At what age do persons begin to be obliged to confession?**
When they come to the use of reason, so as to be capable of mortal sin, which is generally supposed to be about the age of seven years.

[16] Lk 10:16

180. **And at what time do they begin to be obliged to Communion?**
When they are sufficiently capable of being instructed in those sacred mysteries, and of discerning the body of our Lord.

The Sacraments

181. **What is a sacrament?**
An outward sign of inward grace, or a sacred mysterious sign and ceremony ordained by Christ, by which grace is conveyed to our souls.

182. **Do all the sacraments give grace?**
Yes, if we are duly prepared.

183. **Whence have the sacraments the power of giving grace?**
From Christ's precious blood.

184. **Is it a great happiness to receive the sacraments worthily?**
Yes, it is the greatest happiness in the world.

185. **How many sacraments are there?**
These seven: baptism, confirmation, Holy Eucharist, penance, extreme unction, holy order, and matrimony.

BAPTISM

186. **What is baptism?**
It is a sacrament by which we are made Christians, children of God, and heirs of heaven; and are cleansed from original sin, and actual, if we be guilty of any.

187. **How is baptism given?**
By pouring water on the child with the words ordained by Christ.

188. **What are these words?**
"I baptize thee in the name of the Father, and of the Son, and of the Holy Ghost." Which words ought to be said at the same time the water is poured.

189. **What do we promise in baptism?**
To renounce the devil, with all his works and pomps.

CONFIRMATION

190. **What is confirmation?**
It is a sacrament in which, by the imposition of the hands of the bishop, we receive the Holy Ghost, in order to make us strong and perfect Christians and soldiers of Jesus Christ.

191. **How does the bishop administer this sacrament?**
He prays that the Holy Ghost may come down upon us; and makes the sign of the cross with chrism on our foreheads.

THE HOLY EUCHARIST

192. **What is the holy eucharist?**
It is the true body and blood of Christ under the appearance of bread and wine.

193. **Why has Christ given himself to us in this sacrament?**
To feed and nourish our souls, and to enable us to perform all Christian duties.

194. **How is the bread and wine changed into the body and blood of Christ?**
By the power of God, to whom nothing is hard or impossible.

195. **When is this change made?**
When the words of consecration ordained by Jesus Christ are pronounced by the priest in the Mass.

196. **How must we prepare ourselves to receive the Blessed Sacrament?**
We must be in the state of grace, and be fasting from midnight.

197. **Is it a great sin to receive unworthily?**
Yes, it is; for "he that eats and drinks unworthily, eats and drinks judgment to himself."[17]

198. **What is it to receive unworthily?**
To receive in mortal sin.

199. **What is the Mass?**
It is the unbloody sacrifice of the body and blood of Christ.

200. **What are the ends for which we are to offer up this sacrifice?**
First, for God's honor and glory. Secondly, in thanksgiving for all his benefits; and as a perpetual memorial of the passion and death of his Son. Thirdly, for obtaining pardon for our sins. And fourthly, for obtaining all graces and blessing through Jesus Christ.

201. **How must we hear Mass?**
With very great attention and devotion.

PENANCE

202. **What is the sacrament of penance?**
It is a sacrament in which, by the priest's absolution, joined with contrition, confession, and satisfaction, the sins are forgiven which we have committed after baptism.

[17] 1 Cor 11:29

203. **How do you prove that the priest has power to absolve sinners if they be truly penitent?**
From the words of Christ: "Whose sins ye shall forgive, they are forgiven."[18]

204. **What are the parts of penance?**
Contrition, confession, and satisfaction.

205. **What is contrition?**
A hearty sorrow for our sins, by which we have offended so good a God, with a firm purpose of amendment.

206. **What is a firm purpose of amendment?**
It is a resolution, by the grace of God, not only to avoid sin, but also the occasions of it.

207. **Why are we to be sorry for our sins?**
The chiefest and best motive to be sorry for our sins is for the love of God, who is infinitely good in himself and infinitely good to us; and, therefore, we ought to be exceedingly grieved for having offended him.

208. **What other motives have we to be sorry for our sins?**
Because by them we lose heaven and deserve hell.

209. **How may we obtain this hearty contrition and sorrow for our sins?**
We must earnestly beg it of God; and make use of such considerations and mediations as may move us to it.

210. **What is confession?**
It is to accuse ourselves of all our sins to a priest.

[18] Jn 20:23

211. **What if one willfully conceals a mortal sin in confession?**
He commits a great sin, by telling a lie to the Holy Ghost, and makes his confession nothing worth.

212. **What must we do that we may leave out no sins in confession?**
We must carefully examine our conscience upon the ten commandments and the seven deadly sins.

213. **How many things then have we to do by way of preparation for confession?**
Four things. First, we must heartily pray to God for his grace to help us. Secondly, we must carefully examine our conscience. Thirdly, we must beg pardon of God, and be very sorry from our hearts for offending him. And fourthly, we must resolve to renounce our sins and to begin a new life for the future.

214. **What is satisfaction?**
It is doing the penance given by the priest.

215. **What is an indulgence?**
It is a releasing the temporal punishment which often remains due to sin, after the guilt has been remitted by the sacrament of penance.

EXTREME UNCTION

216. **What is extreme unction?**
It is the anointing of the sick, with prayer, for the forgiveness of their sins.

217. **When is this sacrament given?**
When we are in danger of death by sickness.

218. **What scripture have you for this sacrament?**
"Is any one sick among you? Let him bring in the priests of the church and let them pray over him, anointing him with oil in the name of the Lord;

and the prayer of faith shall save the sick man; and the Lord shall raise him up; and if he be in sins, they shall be forgiven him."[19]

HOLY ORDER

219. **What is order?**

It is a sacrament by which bishops, priests, etc., are ordained, and receive grace and power to perform the duties belonging to their charge.

MATRIMONY

220. **What is matrimony?**

It is a sacrament which gives grace to the married couple to love one another, and bring up their children in the fear of God.

Of the Virtues and Vices, etc.

221. **How many are the theological virtues?**

Three: faith, hope, and charity.

222. **What does faith help us to do?**

It helps us to believe, without doubting, all that God has taught and the Church proposes.

223. **What does hope help us to do?**

To put our trust in God, that he will give us all things necessary for our salvation, if we do what he requires of us.

[19] Jas 5:14-15

224. **What does charity help us to do?**
It helps us to love God above all things, and our neighbors as ourselves.

225. **How many are the cardinal virtues?**
Four: prudence, justice, fortitude, and temperance.

226. **How many are the gifts of the Holy Ghost?**
Seven: wisdom, understanding, counsel, fortitude, knowledge, godliness, and the fear of our Lord.

227. **How many are the fruits of the Holy Ghost?**
Twelve: charity, joy, peace, patience, benignity, goodness, longanimity, mildness, faith, modesty, continency, chastity.

228. **Which are the two precepts of charity?**
1) Thou shalt love the Lord thy God, with thy whole heart, with thy whole soul, with all thy strength, and with all thy mind; 2) and thy neighbor as thyself.

229. **Say the seven corporal works of mercy.**

1. To feed the hungry.
2. To give drink to the thirsty.
3. To clothe the naked.
4. To visit and ransom captives.
5. To harbor the harborless.
6. To visit the sick.
7. To bury the dead.

230. **Say the seven spiritual works of mercy.**

1. To convert the sinner.
2. To instruct the ignorant.
3. To counsel the doubtful.
4. To comfort the sorrowful.
5. To bear wrongs patiently.

6. To forgive injuries.
7. To pray for the living and the dead.

231. **Say the eight beatitudes.**

1. Blessed are the poor in spirit, for theirs is the kingdom of heaven.
2. Blessed are the meek, for they shall possess the land.
3. Blessed are they that mourn, for they shall be comforted.
4. Blessed are they that hunger and thirst after righteousness, for they shall be filled.
5. Blessed are the merciful, for they shall find mercy.
6. Blessed are the clean of heart, for they shall see God.
7. Blessed are the peacemakers, for they shall be called the children of God.
8. Blessed are they that suffer persecution for justice' sake, for theirs is the kingdom of heaven.

232. **Say the seven deadly sins.**

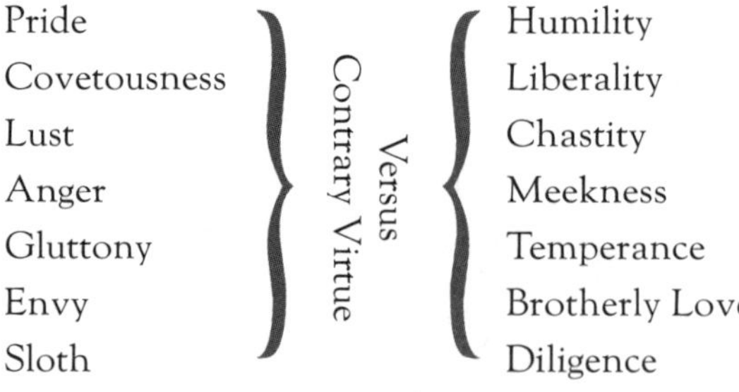

233. **Say the six sins against the Holy Ghost.**

1. Presumption of God's mercy.
2. Despair.
3. Impugning the known truth.
4. Envy at another's spiritual good.
5. Obstinacy in sin.
6. Final impenitence.

234. **Say the four sins crying to heaven for vengeance.**

1. Willful murder.
2. Sodomy.
3. Oppression of the poor.
4. Defrauding laborers of their wages.

235. **Say the nine ways of being accessory to another person's sins.**

1. By counsel.
2. By command.
3. By consent.
4. By provocation.
5. By praise or flattery.
6. By concealment.
7. By partaking.
8. By silence.
9. By defense of the ill done.

236. **Say the three eminent good works.**

1. Prayer.
2. Fasting.
3. Almsdeeds.

237. **Say the evangelical counsels.**

1. Voluntary poverty.
2. Perpetual chastity.
3. Entire obedience.

238. **Say the four last things to be remembered.**

1. Death.
2. Judgment.
3. Hell.
4. Heaven.

The Christian's Rule of Life

239. **Who was the founder of the Christian religion?**
Jesus Christ, the Son of God, who came down from heaven to teach us the way to heaven.

240. **What rule of life then must the Christian follow if he hopes to be saved?**
He must follow the rule of life taught by Jesus Christ.

241. **What is the Christian to do by this rule?**
He must always hate sin, and love God.

242. **How is he to hate sin?**
Above all other evils; so as to be resolved never to commit a willful sin, for the love or fear of anything whatsoever.

243. **How is he to love God?**
Above all things, and with his whole heart.

244. **How is he to learn to love God?**
He must beg of God to teach him: "O my God teach me to love thee!"

245. **What else must he do?**
He must often think how good God is, often speak to him in his heart, and always seek to please him.

246. **And does not Jesus Christ also teach us to love one another?**
Yes; he commands us to love all persons without exception, for his sake.

247. **In what manner are we to love one another?**
In God, and for God, so as to wish well to all; and to pray for all; and never to allow ourselves any thought, word, or deed, to the prejudice of anyone.

248. **And are we also to love our enemies?**
Yes, we are; not only by forgiving them from our hearts, but also by wishing them well, and praying for them.

249. **What other rules does Jesus Christ give to all that desire to be his disciples?**
To deny ourselves, to take up our cross, and to follow him.[20]

250. **What is meant by "denying ourselves"?**
The renouncing our own will, and going against our own humors, inclinations, and passions.

251. **Why are we bound to deny ourselves in this manner?**
Because our natural inclinations are prone to evil from our very childhood, and if not curbed and corrected by self-denial, will infallibly carry us to hell.

252. **What is meant by "taking up our cross"?**
Patiently submitting to and willingly embracing the labors and sufferings of this short life.

253. **And what is meant by "following Christ"?**
To follow Christ is to walk in his footsteps, by an imitation of his virtues.

254. **What are the virtues we are to learn of him?**
To be meek and humble of heart, to be obedient unto death, and to seek to do in all things the will of his Father.

255. **Which are the enemies the Christian must fight against all the days of his life?**
The devil, the world, and the flesh.

256. **Whom do you mean by "the devil"?**
Satan, and all his wicked angels, who are ever seeking to draw us into sin, that we may be damned with them.

[20] Cf. Mt 16:24

257. **Whom do you mean by "the world"?**
All wicked company; and all such as love the vanities, riches, and pleasures of this world better than God.

258. **Why do you number these amongst the enemies of the soul?**
Because they are always seeking by word or example to carry us along with them in the broad road that leads to damnation.

259. **And what do you mean by "the flesh"?**
Our own corrupt inclinations and passions which are the most dangerous of all our enemies.

260. **What must we do to hinder these enemies from dragging us along with them to hell?**
We must always watch, pray, and fight against all their suggestions and temptations.

261. **Whom must we depend upon in this warfare?**
Not upon ourselves, but upon God alone.

The Christian's Daily Exercise

262. **What is the first thing you should do in the morning?**
Make the sign of the cross, and offer my heart and soul to God.

263. **What must you do next?**
Rise diligently, dress myself modestly, and entertain myself with good thoughts; particularly by considering the goodness of God who gives me this day to labor in it for the salvation of my soul; and that perhaps this may be my last.

264. **And what do you do after you have put on your clothes?**
I kneel down to my prayers, and perform my morning exercise.

265. **What is your morning exercise?**
First, I bow down my whole soul and body to adore my God; and I offer myself to his divine service. Secondly, I give him thanks for his infinite goodness to me, and to all his creatures; and desire to join with all the angels and saints in blessing and praising him. Thirdly, I crave pardon from my heart for all my sins; and beg that I may rather die than offend my God anymore. Fourthly, I offer up to God all my thoughts, words, and actions of the day, and beg his blessing on them.

266. **And what prayers do you say after this?**
I say the Our Father, the Hail Mary, and the Apostles' Creed; and I make acts of faith, hope, and love of God.

267. **Do you do anything else?**
I pray for my friends and for my enemies; for the living and for the dead; and I beg mercy, grace, and salvation for all. Then I conclude by desiring our Blessed Lady to be a Mother to me; and by recommending myself to my good angels, and to all the court of heaven.

268. **Is this all a good Christian should do by way of morning exercise?**
No; for he ought also, if he has time and opportunity, to meditate in the morning on his last end, or some other devout subject, and to hear Mass with attention and devotion.

269. **What ought you to do at the beginning of every work or employment?**
I ought to offer it up to God's service, and to think that I will do it because it is his will, and in order to please him.

270. **And what are you to do as to your eating, drinking, sleeping, and diversions?**
All these things I must use with moderation, and do them because such is the will of God; and with a good intention to please him.

271. **By what other means must you sanctify your ordinary actions and employments of the day?**
By often raising up my heart to God whilst I am about them, and saying some short prayer to him.

272. **What do you do as often as you hear the clock strike?**
I turn myself to God, and I say to him, "O my God, teach me to love thee in time and eternity."

273. **What do you do as often as you receive any blessing from God?**
I endeavor immediately to make him a return of thanksgiving and love.

274. **And what do you do when you find yourself tempted to sin?**
I make the sign of the cross upon my heart, and I call upon God as earnestly as I can, "Lord save me or I perish!"

275. **And what if you have fallen into any sin?**
I cast myself in spirit at the feet of Christ, and humbly beg his pardon saying, "Lord be merciful to me a sinner."

276. **And what do you say when God sends you any cross, or suffering, or sickness, or pain?**
I say, "Lord, thy will be done; I take this for my sins."

277. **And what other little prayers do you say to yourself, from time to time, in the day?**
Lord, what wilt thou have me to do? O teach me to do thy holy will in all things. Lord keep me from sin. May the name of our Lord be forever blessed. Come, my dear Jesus, and take full possession of my soul. Glory be to the Father, and to the Son, and to the Holy Ghost. As it was in the beginning, is now, and ever shall be, world without end. Amen.

278. **What is your evening exercise?**
I say the Our Father, the Hail Mary, and Belief,[21] together with the acts of faith, hope, and love of God, etc., as I did in the morning.

279. **And do not you always join with the family in saying the litanies and other evening prayers which are usually said in Catholic families?**
Yes; as also in the daily examination of conscience.

280. **How do you make this daily examination of conscience?**
First, I place myself in the presence of God, (as I usually do at the beginning of all my prayers) and I beg his light and help to know my sins, and to be sorry for them.

Secondly, I consider how I have spent the day from morning till night, in what manner I have performed my prayers and all other duties; what blessings I have received from God; and what offenses I have been guilty of against him, by commission or omission.

Thirdly, I give thanks to God for all his blessings; and beg pardon for all my sins, endeavoring to make a hearty act of contrition for them.

Fourthly, I commend my soul into the hands of God, with the best dispositions I can of love, and conformity to his blessed will, as I were to die that night.

281. **How do you finish the day?**
I observe due modesty in going to bed; entertaining myself with the thoughts of death; and I endeavor to compose myself to rest at the foot of the cross; and to give my last thoughts to my crucified Savior.

282. **How do you make an act of faith?**
O eternal truth, who hast revealed thyself to me, one God in three Persons, Father, Son, and Holy Ghost, I believe in thee, O Jesus Christ, the Son of God, my Savior and Redeemer who hast died for us all, I believe in thee. I believe all the divine truths which thou, my God, hast taught us by thy word and by thy Church, because thou hast taught them, who are the sovereign truth; and I had rather die than call in question any of these truths.

[21] Editor's note: Creed.

283. **How do you make an act of hope?**
O my God, who art infinitely powerful, and infinitely good and merciful, who hast made me for thyself, and redeemed me by the blood of thy Son, and promised us all good through him; I firmly hope for mercy, grace, and salvation from thee, through the same Jesus Christ my Savior; resolving on my part, to do all that thou requirest of me.

284. **How do you make an act of the love of God?**
O my God and my all, infinitely good in thyself, and infinitely good to me, I desire to praise thee, bless thee, and glorify thee forever. O take possession of my whole soul, and make me forever a servant of thy love.

285. **And how do you make an act of the love of your neighbors?**
O my God, thou hast commended me to love every neighbor as myself for thy sake; O give me grace to fulfill this commandment. I desire to love every neighbor, whether friend or enemy, in thee, and for thee. I renounce every thought, word, or deed that is contrary to this love. I forgive all that have any way offended me; and beg thy mercy, grace, and salvation for all the world.

286. **How do you make an act of contrition for your sins?**
O my God, who art infinitely good, and always hatest sin; I beg pardon from the bottom of my heart for all my offenses against thee; I detest them all, and am heartily sorry for them, because they offend thy infinite goodness, and I beg I may rather die than be guilty of them anymore.

The Manner of Lay Persons Baptizing an Infant in Case of Danger of Death

Take common water, pour it on the head or face of the child, and while you are pouring it say the following words:

"I baptize thee in the name of the Father, and of the Son, and of the Holy Ghost. Amen."

Note.—Any person, whether man, woman, or child may baptize an infant in case of danger of death.

PRAYERS FOR MORNING

In the name of the Father, and of the Son, and of the Holy Ghost. Amen.

Blessed be the Holy and undivided Trinity, now and forever. Amen.

O Almighty God, I humbly adore thy majesty, and with all the powers of my soul I praise thy holy name for the infinite blessings thou hast so freely bestowed on me, and particularly for thy gracious protection from the dangers of this night. I humbly beg thy grace through the death and passion of Jesus Christ, that I may not fall into any sin this day, and especially that I may be preserved from such faults which I am most subject to. I resolve to renounce them forever, O my God, and, to the best of my power, to fly all dangerous occasions. But of myself I can do nothing, and therefore my whole trust and confidence is in thy goodness and mercy, and in the assistance of thy divine grace.

Our Father, etc.[22]

Hail Mary, etc.[23]

I believe in God, etc.[24]

The acts of faith, hope, charity, and contrition.

The Confiteor

I confess to Almighty God, to Blessed Mary ever Virgin, to blessed Michael the archangel, to blessed John the Baptist, to the holy apostles Peter and Paul, and to all the saints, that I have sinned exceedingly in thought, word, and deed, through my fault, through my fault, through my most grievous fault: therefore, I beseech the Blessed Mary ever Virgin, the blessed Michael the archangel, the blessed John the Baptist, the holy apostles Peter and Paul, and all the saints to pray to the Lord our God for me.

May the Almighty God have mercy on me, and forgive me my sins, and bring me to everlasting life. Amen.

[22] See p. 18, above.
[23] See p. 19, above.
[24] See p. 7, above.

Grant, O Lord, that I may serve thee this day in spirit and truth by faith, hope, and love; give me prudence to direct my steps to thee, justice to regulate my conduct to my neighbors, fortitude to carry me safe through all difficulties and dangers, and temperance to restrain me from all unlawful pleasures and passions; teach me to be meek and humble of heart, and to deny myself; teach me in all things to know and to do thy holy will. Amen.

O Almighty and eternal God, grant to us the increase of faith, hope, and charity; and that we may deserve to obtain what thou promisest, make us to love what thou commandest, through Christ our Lord. Amen.

PRAYERS FOR NIGHT

In the name of the Father, and of the Son, and of the Holy Ghost. Amen.

Blessed be the Holy and undivided Trinity now and forever. Amen.

O eternal God, whose majesty filleth heaven and earth, I firmly believe thou art here, that thou seest and knowest all things, and art most intimately present in the very center of my soul. I desire to bow down all the powers of my soul to adore thee, praise thee, and glorify thee now and forever. I give thee thanks from the bottom of my heart for all the mercies and blessings I have received from thee this day, in thy watching over me, and preserving me from so many evils, and favoring me with so many graces.

Our Father, etc. Hail Mary, etc. I believe in God, etc. The acts of faith, hope, charity, and contrition, and the *confiteor*, as in the morning prayers.

Receive me, O Lord, I beseech thee, into thy protection, and let the eye of thy providence watch over me this night to come; grant that when my body is asleep, my soul may be awake to thee; that thy holy angels, to whose care I am committed by the supreme clemency, may enlighten, govern, and defend me from all sins and dangers. Grant that by preserving in the duties of thy service, I may end my days in thy favor, and rejoice with thee forever in thy heavenly kingdom. Amen.

O Almighty and eternal God, grant to us the increase of faith, hope, and charity; and, that we may deserve to obtain what thou promisest, make us to love what thou commandest. Through Christ our Lord. Amen.

AN

ABRIDGMENT

OF THE

QUEBEC

CATECHISM.

REVISED, AND AUTHORISED BY HIS LORDSHIP THE RT. REV. JOS. SIGNAY, BISHOP OF QUEBEC.

QUEBEC.

Printed and sold by J. B. FRÉCHETTE & Co., No. 25, Mountain Street.

1834.

Original Title Page

AN

ABRIDGMENT

OF THE

QUEBEC

CATECHISM.

Revised, and authorised by His Lordship the Rt. Rev. Jos. Signay, Bishop of Quebec.

QUEBEC.

Printed and sold by J. B. Fréchette & Co., No. 25, Mountain Street.

1834.

JOSEPH SIGNAY,

Catholic Bishop of Quebec, etc., etc., etc.

We have seen and examined the present edition of the *Abridgment of the Quebec Catechism*, and we authorize the use thereof, conformably to the mandate of His Lordship B. C. Panet, the late bishop of Quebec, bearing date the 2nd of March, 1829, and inserted at the head of the large diocesan catechism published the same year.

Given at Quebec, the 20th of February, 1834.

✠ Jos. Cath. Bishop of Quebec.

MORNING AND EVENING PRAYERS
To Be Taught to Children, in Their Mother Tongue at Least

The Sign of the Cross

✠ *In nomine Patris, et Filii, et Spiritus Sancti. Amen.*

✠ In the name of the Father, and of the Son, and of the Holy Ghost. Amen.

The Lord's Prayer

Pater Noster qui es in coelis.

1. *Sanctificetur nomen tuum.*
2. *Adveniat regnum tuum.*
3. *Fiat voluntas tua, sicut in coelo et in terra.*
4. *Panem nostrum quotidianum da nobis hodie.*
5. *Et dimitte nobis debita nostra, sicut et nos dimittimus debitoribus nostris.*
6. *Et ne nos inducas in tentationem.*
7. *Sed libera nos a malo. Amen.*

Our Father who art in heaven.

1. Hallowed be thy name.
2. Thy kingdom come.
3. Thy will be done on earth, as it is in heaven.
4. Give us this day our daily bread.
5. And forgive us our trespasses, as we forgive them that trespass against us.
6. And lead us not into temptation.
7. But deliver us from evil. Amen.

The Angelical Salutation

Ave Maria, gratia plena, Dominus tecum: benedicta tu in mulieribus, et benedictus fructus ventris tui, Jesus.

Sancta Maria, Mater Dei, ora pro nobis peccatoribus, nunc et in hora mortis nostrae. Amen.

Hail Mary, full of grace, the Lord is with thee: blessed art thou amongst women, and blessed is the fruit of thy womb, Jesus.

Holy Mary, Mother of God, pray for us sinners, now and at the hour of our death. Amen.

The Apostles' Creed

1. *Credo in Deum Patrem omnipotentem, Creatorem coeli et terrae.*
2. *Et in Jesum Christum Filium ejus unicum, Dominum nostrum.*
3. *Qui conceptus est de Spiritu Sancto, natus ex Maria Virgine.*
4. *Passus sub Pontio Pilato, crucifixus, mortuus, et sepultus.*
5. *Descendit ad inferos, tertia die resurrexit a mortuis.*
6. *Ascendit ad coelos, sedet ad dexteram Dei Patris omnipotentis.*
7. *Inde venturus est judicare vivos et mortuos.*
8. *Credo in Spiritum Sanctum.*
9. *Sanctam Ecclesiam Catholicam, sanctorum communionem.*
10. *Remissionem peccatorum.*
11. *Carnis resurrectionem.*
12. *Vitam aeternam. Amen.*

1. I believe in God, the Father Almighty, Creator of heaven and earth.
2. And in Jesus Christ his only Son our Lord.
3. Who was conceived by the Holy Ghost, born of the Virgin Mary.
4. Suffered under Pontius Pilate, was crucified, dead, and buried.
5. He descended into hell, the third day he rose again from the dead.
6. He ascended into heaven, sits at the right hand of God, the Father Almighty.
7. From thence he shall come to judge the living and the dead.
8. I believe in the Holy Ghost.
9. The holy Catholic Church, the communion of saints.
10. The forgiveness of sins.
11. The resurrection of the body.
12. And the life everlasting. Amen.

The Confiteor

Confiteor Deo omnipotenti, Beatae Mariae semper Virgini, beato Michaeli archangelo, beato Joanni Baptistae, sanctis apostolis Petro et Paula, et omnibus sanctis, (et tibi, Pater,) quia peccavi nimis cogitatione, verbo, et opere, mea culpa, mea culpa, mea maxima culpa. Ideo precor Beatam Mariam semper Virginem, beatum Michaelem archangelum, beatum Joannem Baptistam, sanctos apostolos Petrum et Paulum, et omnes sanctos, (et te, Pater,) orare pro me ad Dominum Deum nostrum.

Misereatur nostri omnipotens Deus, et dimissis peccatis nostris, perducat nos ad vitam aeternam. Amen.

Indulgentiam, absolutionem, et remissionem peccatorum nostrorum tribuat nobis omnipotens et misericors Dominus. Amen.

I confess to Almighty God, to Blessed Mary ever Virgin, to blessed Michael the archangel, to blessed John the Baptist, to the holy apostles Peter and Paul, and to all the saints, (and to you, Father,) that I have grievously sinned in thought, word, and deed, through my fault, through my fault, through my exceeding great fault. Therefore, I beseech Blessed Mary ever Virgin, blessed Michael the archangel, blessed John the Baptist, the holy apostles Peter and Paul, and all the saints, (and you, Father,) to pray to the Lord our God for me.

May the Almighty God have mercy on us, forgive us our sins, and bring us to everlasting life. Amen.

May the Almighty and merciful Lord give us pardon, absolution, and remission of our sins. Amen.

Act of Adoration

O my God, I adore thee and acknowledge thee for my Creator and sovereign Lord, and the absolute master of all things.

Act of Faith

O my God, I firmly believe all that the holy Catholic Church believes and teaches, because thou, who art truth itself, hast revealed it.

Act of Hope

O my God, relying upon thy promises and upon the merits of my Savior, I hope with a firm confidence that thou wilt grant me grace to observe thy commandments in this world, and to be rewarded in the next.

Act of Love or Charity

O my God, who art worthy of all love, for thy infinite perfections, I love thee with my whole heart, and I love my neighbor as myself for the love of thee.

Act of Contrition

O my God, I am heartily sorry for having offended thee, because thou art infinitely good and infinitely amiable, because sin is displeasing to thee; pardon me through the merits of Jesus Christ my Savior; I propose, with the help of thy holy grace, never more to offend thee, and to do penance.

Act of Thanksgiving

O my God, I thank thee for all the good I have received from thee, particularly for having created and redeemed me by thy Son, and made me a child of thy Church.

Act of Oblation

O my God, I have received all from thee; to thee I offer my thoughts, words, and actions, my life and all that I possess, and I desire to employ it in thy service alone.

Act of Humility

O my God, who resistest the proud and givest grace to the humble, suppress in me all motions of pride, and teach me to despise myself, who am but dust and ashes.

Act of Demand

O my God, infinite source of all good, give me whatever is necessary for the life and health of the body, but especially grace to do thy holy will in all things. Through Jesus Christ our Lord. Amen.

The Ten Commandments of God

I am the Lord thy God who brought thee out of the Land of Egypt, out of the house of bondage.

1. Thou shalt not have strange gods before me; thou shalt not make to thyself a graven thing, nor the likeness of any thing that is in heaven above, or in the earth below, nor of things that are in the waters under the earth: thou shalt not adore nor worship them: I am the Lord thy God, strong, jealous, visiting the sins of the fathers upon the children, to the third and fourth generation of them that hate me: and showing mercy to thousands of those that love me, and keep my commandments.
2. Thou shalt not take the name of the Lord thy God in vain: for the Lord will not hold him guiltless that shall take his name in vain.
3. Remember to keep holy the sabbath day.
4. Honor thy father and thy mother.
5. Thou shalt not kill.
6. Thou shalt not commit adultery.
7. Thou shalt not steal.
8. Thou shalt not bear false witness against thy neighbor.
9. Thou shalt not covet thy neighbor's wife.
10. Thou shalt not covet thy neighbor's goods.[1]

[1] Cf. Ex 20

The Seven Commandments of the Church

1. To keep holy all festivals of obligation.
2. To hear Mass on Sundays and holy days.
3. To confess our sins, at least once a year.
4. Worthily to receive the Holy Eucharist about Easter.
5. To fast Lent, Ember days, and vigils commanded.
6. To abstain from flesh meat all Fridays and Saturdays.
7. To pay tithes to our pastors.

In Honor of the Holy Trinity

Gloria Patri, et Filio, et Spiritui Sancto.

Sicut erat in principio, et nunc, et semper, et in saecula saeculorum. Amen.

Glory be to the Father, and to the Son, and to the Holy Ghost.

As it was in the beginning, is now, and ever shall be, world without end. Amen.

A Prayer to the Holy Virgin

Sub tuum praesidium confugimus, sancta Dei Genitrix: nostras deprecationes ne despicias in necessitatibus; sed a periculis cunctis libera nos semper, Virgo gloriosa et benedicta. Amen.

We fly to thy patronage, O holy Mother of God: despise not our prayers in our necessities; but deliver us always from all dangers, O glorious and blessed Virgin. Amen.

A Prayer to Our Guardian Angel

Angele Dei, qui custos es mei, me tibi commissum pietate superna, hodie illumina, custodi, rege, et guberna. Amen.

O angel of God, to whose holy care I am committed, enlighten, defend, and keep me this day from all sin and danger. Amen.

Grace before Meat

Benedicite, Dominus. Nos et ea quae sumus sumpturi benedicat dextera Christi. Amen.

In nomine Patris, etc.

Bless us, O Lord, and these thy gifts, which of thy bounty we are about to receive: through Christ our Lord. Amen.

In the name of the Father, etc.

Grace after Meat

Agimus tibi gratias, omnipotens Deus, pro universis beneficiis tuis; qui vivis et regnas in saecula saeculorum. Amen.

In nomine Patris, etc.

We give thee thanks, O Almighty God, for all thy benefits; who livest and reignest, world without end. Amen.

In the name of the Father, etc.

A Prayer for the Dead

Fidelium animae, per misericordiam Dei requiescant in pace. Amen.

May the souls of the faithful departed through the mercy of God rest in peace. Amen.

The Angelus Domini

℣. *Angelus Domini nuntiavit Mariae.*
℟. *Et concepit de Spiritu Sancto.*
Ave Maria, etc.
℣. *Ecce ancilla Domini.*
℟. *Fiat mihi secundum verbum tuum.*
Ave Maria, etc.

℣. *Et verbum caro factum est.*

℟. *Et habitavit in nobis.*

Ave Maria, etc.

℣. *Ora, pro nobis, sancta Dei Genitrix.*

℟. *Ut digni efficiamur promissionibus Christi.*

Oremus.

Gratiam tuam quaesumus, Domine, mentibus nostris infunde, ut, qui angelo nuntiante, Christi Filii tui incarnationem cognovimus, per passionem ejus et crucem ad resurrectionis gloriam perducamur: per eumdem Christum Dominum nostrum.

℟. *Amen.*

℣. The angel of the Lord declared unto Mary.

℟. And she conceived of the Holy Ghost.

Hail Mary, etc.

℣. Behold the handmaid of the Lord:

℟. Be it done unto me according to thy word.

Hail Mary, etc.

℣. And the Word was made flesh.

℟. And dwelt among us.

Hail Mary, etc.

℣. Pray for us, O holy Mother of God.

℟. That we may be made worthy of the promises of Christ.

Let us pray.

Pour forth, we beseech thee, O Lord, thy grace unto our hearts, that we, to whom the incarnation of Christ, thy Son, was made known by the message of an angel, may, by his passion and cross, be brought to the glory of his resurrection: through the same Christ our Lord.

℟. Amen.

Abridgment of the Catechism

Note.—For children, and even for adults of little capacity, the questions preceded by this sign * may suffice. The other questions are not above the capacity of children in general, who are preparing either for their first Communion, or for confirmation, whether they can read or not.

Preliminary Questions

* 1. **Are you a Christian?**
Yes, by the grace of God.

2. **By what were you made a Christian?**
By baptism.

* 3. **What is the mark of a Christian?**
The sign of the cross.

* 4. **Make the sign of the cross.**
✠ In the name of the Father, and of the Son, and of the Holy Ghost. Amen.

Of the Mysteries

5. **What do you mean by the word *mystery*?**
By the word *mystery*, I mean a truth that we do not comprehend, but which nevertheless we are obliged to believe, because God has revealed it.

6. **Which are the principal mysteries of our religion?**
The principal mysteries of our religion are those of the Holy Trinity, of the incarnation, and of the redemption.

* 7. **What is the mystery of the Holy Trinity?**
One God in three Persons, Father, Son, and Holy Ghost.

* 8. **What is the mystery of the incarnation?**
The Son of God made man for us.

* 9. **What is the mystery of the redemption?**
Jesus Christ crucified for us.

10. **Where are those mysteries to be found?**
In the Creed or Symbol of the Apostles.

Of the Apostles' Creed

* 11. **Say the Apostles' Creed.**
In English:
1. I believe in God, the Father Almighty, Creator of heaven and earth.
2. And in Jesus Christ his only Son our Lord.
3. Who was conceived by the Holy Ghost, born of the Virgin Mary.
4. Suffered under Pontius Pilate, was crucified, dead, and buried.
5. He descended into hell, the third day he rose again from the dead.
6. He ascended into heaven, sits at the right hand of God, the Father Almighty.
7. From thence he shall come to judge the living and the dead.
8. I believe in the Holy Ghost.
9. The holy Catholic Church, the communion of saints.

10. The forgiveness of sins.
11. The resurrection of the body.
12. And the life everlasting. Amen.

In Latin:

1. *Credo in Deum Patrem omnipotentem, Creatorem coeli et terrae.*
2. *Et in Jesum Christum Filium ejus unicum, Dominum nostrum.*
3. *Qui conceptus est de Spiritu Sancto, natus ex Maria Virgine.*
4. *Passus sub Pontio Pilato, crucifixus, mortuus, et sepultus.*
5. *Descendit ad inferos, tertia die resurrexit a mortuis.*
6. *Ascendit ad coelos, sedet ad dexteram Dei Patris omnipotentis.*
7. *Inde venturus est judicare vivos et mortuos.*
8. *Credo in Spiritum Sanctum.*
9. *Sanctam Ecclesiam Catholicam, sanctorum communionem.*
10. *Remissionem peccatorum.*
11. *Carnis resurrectionem.*
12. *Vitam aeternam.* Amen.

12. **What means the word *I believe*?**

It means: "I hold for certain, I am fully persuaded, I am entirely convinced."

ARTICLE 1

13. **Which is the first article of the Apostles' Creed?**

I believe in God, the Father Almighty, Creator of heaven and earth.

* 14. **What is God?**

God is a Spirit infinitely perfect.

* 15. **Can there be many gods, or many spirits infinitely perfect?**

No; there can be but one alone.

* 16. **Where is God?**

God is everywhere; he fills heaven and earth.

17. **Why do you say, "I believe in God the Father"?**
To show that the first Person in God is called the Father.

18. **Are there several Persons in God?**
Yes; in God there are three Persons, the Father, the Son, and the Holy Ghost.

* 19. **Is each of these three Persons, God?**
Yes; each of these three Persons is God.

* 20. **Are these three Persons equal in all things?**
Yes; they are equal in all things.

* 21. **There are therefore three gods?**
No; the three divine Persons are only one and the same God.

* 22. **How so?**
Because they have but one and the same divine nature.

* 23. **How is the mystery of one only God in three Persons, Father, Son, and Holy Ghost, called?**
It is called "the mystery of the Holy Trinity."

24. **Why is God, in the first article of the Creed, called "Almighty"?**
Because nothing is impossible to Him.

* 25. **Does God see and know all things?**
Yes; God sees and knows all things, even the most hidden thoughts of our heart.

* 26. **Has God always been and will he always be?**
Yes; for he is eternal.

27. **Why do you call him, "Creator of heaven and earth"?**
Because he created and made all things out of nothing; and because he is the absolute master thereof.

* 28. **Was it God that created you and brought you into the world?**
Yes; it was God that created me and brought me into the world.

* 29. **Why did God create you?**
That I might know, love, and serve him, and thereby obtain everlasting life.

ARTICLE 2

30. **What do you mean by the second article of the Creed, "And in Jesus Christ, his only Son, our Lord"?**
I mean that God the Father has begotten, from all eternity, an only Son, who is equal to him in all things.

31. **Is the Son of God also called the divine Word, and the second Person of the Holy Trinity?**
Yes; he is.

32. **Is God the Son of the same nature as God the Father?**
Yes; he is consubstantial to the Father, that is to say, of one and the same substance with him.

33. **How is the Son of God made man called?**
He is called "Jesus Christ our Lord."

* 34. **Is Jesus Christ only man?**
No; he is both God and man.

* 35. **There are therefore two natures in Jesus Christ?**
Yes; there is the divine and the human nature.

36. **Are there two Persons in Jesus Christ?**
No; there is but one Person, which is that of the Son of God, or the second Person of the Holy Trinity.

37. **Was Jesus Christ always man?**
No; it was about four thousand years after the creation of the world that the Son of God, who existed from all eternity, was made man and called "Jesus."

38. **What is meant by "being made man"?**
The meaning is that he took a body and soul like ours.

39. **Why was the Son of God made man?**
To redeem us.

40. **From what did he redeem us?**
From eternal damnation, to which we were all condemned by the disobedience of our first father Adam.

41. **How is the mystery of the Son of God made man for us, called?**
It is called "the mystery of the incarnation."

ARTICLE 3

42. **What is meant by the third article of the Symbol, "Who was conceived by the Holy Ghost, born of the Virgin Mary"?**
By the third article is meant that Jesus Christ was conceived by the operation of the Holy Ghost in the womb of a Virgin, named Mary, and that of her he was born into the world.

* 43. **On what day was Jesus Christ born?**
He was born on Christmas day.

44. **How long did Christ remain visible on earth?**
About thirty-three years.

* 45. **What did Jesus Christ do upon earth?**
He taught mankind to lead a holy life, and by his merits, procured them grace to that effect.

ARTICLE 4

46. **Which is the fourth article of the Creed?**
Suffered under Pontius Pilate, was crucified, dead, and buried.

* 47. **What did Jesus Christ suffer?**
He was insulted, despised, scourged, crowned with thorns, and abandoned by all men.

48. **Who was Pontius Pilate?**
He was the governor of Judea, under whom Jesus Christ suffered.

* 49. **Why do you add, "Was crucified, dead, and buried"?**
Because Jesus Christ was nailed to a cross, upon which he expired, and was afterwards laid in the tomb.

* 50. **What is death?**
Death is the separation of the soul from the body.

* 51. **On what day did Jesus Christ suffer death?**
On Good Friday.

* 52. **How is the mystery of the death of Christ upon the cross for us called?**
The mystery of the redemption.

ARTICLE 5

53. **What do you mean by the fifth article of the Creed, "He descended into hell"?**
I mean that the soul of Jesus Christ, after his death, descended into that place of rest called limbo, where the souls of the just, who had died since the creation of the world, were detained.

54. **Why did Jesus Christ descend to limbo?**
To announce to them their delivery, which was the fruit of his sufferings and death.

55. **Why do you add, "The third day he rose again from the dead"?**
Because Jesus Christ rose again, and came living out of the grave, the third day after his death.

56. **What is meant by the word *resurrection*?**
The reunion of the soul with the body.

* 57. **On what day did our Lord rise from the dead?**
On Easter Sunday.

ARTICLE 6

58. **What is meant by the sixth article of the Creed, "He ascended into heaven, sits at the right hand of God, the Father Almighty"?**
It signifies that Jesus Christ, after his resurrection, ascended into heaven in body and soul to reign gloriously at the right hand of his Father; that is to say, to hold, as man, the first place near him.

* 59. **On what day did Jesus Christ ascend into heaven?**
On Ascension day, the fortieth after his resurrection.

* 60. **Where is Jesus Christ at present?**
Jesus Christ, as God, is everywhere; as man, he is in heaven, and in the Blessed Sacrament.

61. **What does Jesus Christ do in heaven?**
Jesus Christ, in heaven, as man, adores God the Father, and intercedes for us; as God, he sends us from thence his Holy Spirit and his graces.

62. **On what day did Jesus Christ send, in a particular manner, the Holy Ghost to his Church?**
On Whitsunday, the tenth day after his ascension.

ARTICLE 7

* 63. **Is Jesus Christ to come again upon earth?**
Yes; Jesus Christ will come upon earth, at the end of the world, for the general judgment, as we learn from the seventh article of the Creed: "From thence he shall come to judge the living and the dead."

* 64. **Is the general judgment the only one we shall have to undergo?**
No; it will be preceded by the particular judgment.

* 65. **When will the particular judgment take place?**
Immediately after death.

66. **When shall we die?**
When it will please God.

* 67. **What will become of our body after death?**
It will return into dust.

68. **And what will become of our soul?**
It will immediately appear before God to be judged.

69. **On what will it be judged?**
On the good or evil it shall have done while in this life.

70. **What will become of the soul after the particular judgment?**
It will go either to heaven, or to hell, or to purgatory, according to its merits.

ARTICLE 8

71. **What do you mean by the eighth article of the Creed, "I believe in the Holy Ghost"?**
By this article we are taught to believe that in God, besides the Father and the Son, there is a third Person called "the Holy Ghost."

* 72. **Is the Holy Ghost God, as well as the Father and the Son?**
Yes; he is equal to them in all things.

ARTICLE 9

73. **Say the ninth article of the Creed.**
The holy Catholic Church, the communion of saints.

The Catholic Church

* 74. **What is the Catholic Church?**
The Catholic Church is the society of the faithful, united together by the profession of the same faith, the participation of the same sacraments, and the submission to the same lawful pastors.

75. **Where is that society to be found which you call "the Church"?**
Wherever there are Catholics.

* 76. **Who established the Church?**
Jesus Christ, who is the invisible head thereof.

77. **Who enlightens and governs it?**
The Holy Ghost.

* 78. **Who are its lawful pastors?**
The pope, the bishops, and the priests who have received their ordination and mission from them.

79. **What do you mean by our holy father "the pope"?**
By "the pope," I mean the bishop of Rome, the first of bishops, the successor of Saint Peter, the center of Catholic unity, and the visible head of the Church.

* 80. **Are there many Catholic Churches?**
No; there is but one Catholic Church, which is the Roman Church, out of which there is no salvation.

81. **What is to be thought of those societies calling themselves "Churches," that do not profess the same faith with us, nor submit to the same pastors?**
They are but human institutions, which only serve to mislead men, and can never conduct them to God.

The Communion of Saints

82. **What do you mean by "the communion of saints"?**
I mean the communication that exists among all the members of the Catholic Church.

83. **In what does that communication or communion consist?**
The communion of saints consists in this: that all the spiritual advantages of the Church are common to all the faithful.

84. **Do we communicate with the saints in heaven?**
Yes; we beseech them to intercede for us with God.

85. **Are we in communion with the souls in purgatory?**
Yes; we offer up our prayers, our good works, and the Holy Sacrifice of the Mass to God for their delivery.

* 86. **What is purgatory?**
Purgatory is a place of punishment, where some souls suffer for a time before they can enter paradise.

ARTICLE 10

87. **What do you mean by the tenth article of the Creed, "The forgiveness of sins"?**
I mean that Jesus Christ has given to his Church the power of remitting sins.

On Sin in General

* 88. **What is sin?**
A disobedience to God.

89. **Are there several kinds of sins?**
Yes; original and actual sin.

* 90. **What is original sin?**
Original sin is that which we bring with us into the world, and of which we became guilty by the disobedience of our first parents.

* 91. **How is original sin remitted?**
By the sacrament of baptism.

92. **Does baptism remit original sin only?**
It also remits all the actual sins committed before its reception.

* 93. **What is actual sin?**
That which we commit by our own free will.

94. **How are actual sins, committed after baptism, forgiven?**
By the sacrament of penance.

* 95. **Are all actual sins the same?**
No; some kill the soul by depriving it of sanctifying grace, and are called "mortal sins"; others merely weaken, but do not destroy sanctifying grace, and are called "venial sins."

96. **How many mortal sins are necessary to deserve hell?**
One only.

The Capital Sins

97. **How many capital sins are there?**
There are seven: pride, avarice, luxury, envy, gluttony, anger, and sloth.

98. **Why are they called "capital"?**
Because they are the source of all other sins.

99. **What is pride?**
Pride is an inordinate esteem of ourselves, which leads us to despise others.

100. **What is avarice?**
Avarice is an inordinate love of earthly things.

101. **What is luxury?**
Luxury is an inordinate love of carnal pleasures.

102. **What is envy?**
Envy is a sadness at another's good.

103. **What is gluttony?**
Gluttony is an inordinate love of eating or drinking.

104. **How is the sin of gluttony most frequently committed?**
By immoderate use of intoxicating liquors; this is what is called "drunkenness."

105. **What means should be taken to avoid the sin of drunkenness?**
Two principal ones: 1) never to go into a tavern without necessity; 2) to take no intoxicating liquors between meals.

106. **What is anger?**
Anger is a violent motion of the soul, urging us to seek revenge.

107. **What is sloth?**
Sloth is a voluntary dislike of labor, and a willful neglect of the duties of our calling.

ARTICLE 11

108. **What is signified by the eleventh article of the Creed, "The resurrection of the body"?**
It signifies that, at the end of the world, all the dead will arise to appear at the general judgment.

109. **Why will the dead arise again?**
To receive in their bodies the reward of their good works or the punishment of their sins.

ARTICLE 12

110. **What is "life everlasting," expressed in the last article of the Creed?**
It is a life which will never end.

111. **Will this life be happy or unhappy?**
It will be infinitely happy in heaven, or infinitely unhappy in hell.

* 112. **What is heaven?**
Heaven is a place of bliss, where, seeing and loving God, we shall enjoy eternal happiness.

* 113. **Who are those who go to heaven?**
Those who have not offended God or who, after having offended him, have done penance.

* 114. **What is hell?**
Hell is a place of torments, where the wicked shall be eternally punished with devils.

* 115. **Who are the wicked who go to hell?**
Those who die in mortal sin.

The Commandments

* 116. **What must we do to obtain heaven?**
We must keep the commandments of God and of the Church.

OF THE COMMANDMENTS OF GOD

* 117. **How many are the commandments of God?**
Ten.

* 118. **Say the ten commandments.**
I am the Lord thy God who brought thee out of the land of Egypt, out of the house of bondage.

1. Thou shalt not have strange gods before me; thou shalt not make to thyself a graven thing, nor the likeness of any thing that is in heaven

above, or in the earth below, nor of things that are in the waters under the earth: thou shalt not adore nor worship them: I am the Lord thy God, strong, jealous, visiting the sins of the fathers upon the children, to the third and fourth generation of them that hate me: and showing mercy to thousands of those that love me, and keep my commandments.

2. Thou shalt not take the name of the Lord thy God in vain: for the Lord will not hold him guiltless that shall take his name in vain.
3. Remember to keep holy the sabbath day.
4. Honor thy father and thy mother.
5. Thou shalt not kill.
6. Thou shalt not commit adultery.
7. Thou shalt not steal.
8. Thou shalt not bear false witness against thy neighbor.
9. Thou shalt not covet thy neighbor's wife.
10. Thou shalt not covet thy neighbor's goods.[2]

* 119. **Give me an abridgment of the ten commandments?**
An abridgment of the ten commandments is contained in these few words: "Thou shalt love the Lord thy God with thy whole heart, and thy neighbor as thyself, for the love of God."

The First Commandment of God

120. **Say the first commandment.**
"I am the Lord thy God,...thou shalt not have strange gods before me."[3]

121. **What are we commanded by the first precept of the decalogue?**
We are commanded: 1) to believe in God; 2) to hope in him; 3) to love him with all our heart; 4) to adore him alone.

[2] Cf. Ex 20
[3] Ex 20:2-3

122. **By what virtue do we believe in God?**
By the virtue of faith.

* 123. **By what virtue do we hope in God?**
By the virtue of hope.

* 124. **Which is the virtue that makes us love God with all our heart?**
The virtue of charity.

* 125. **How are those three virtues called?**
They are called "theological virtues."

* 126. **Make an act of faith.**
Act of faith.—"O my God, I firmly believe all that the holy Catholic Church believes and teaches, because thou, who art truth itself, hast revealed it."

* 127. **Make an act of hope.**
Act of hope.—"O my God, relying upon thy promises and upon the merits of my Savior, I hope with a firm confidence that thou wilt grant me grace to observe thy commandments in this world, and to be rewarded in the next."

* 128. **Make an act of charity.**
Act of charity.—"O my God, who art worthy of all love, for thy infinite perfections, I love thee with my whole heart, and I love my neighbor as myself for the love of thee."

* 129. **Make also an act of adoration.**
Act of adoration.—"O my God, I adore thee and acknowledge thee for my Creator and sovereign Lord, and the absolute master of all things."

* 130. **Is it lawful to adore anything besides God?**
No; to God alone the supreme homage of our hearts and minds is due.

131. **Do we not adore the saints?**
No; we only revere and invoke them, as the friends of God.

132. **Is not the invocation of the saints injurious to the mediation of Jesus Christ?**
No, by no means; because it is always through Jesus Christ that the prayers of the saints and ours are presented to God.

* 133. **Is it lawful to honor the relics and images of the saints?**
Yes; and this has always been practiced in the Catholic Church.

134. **What advantages do we derive from honoring the relics and images of the saints?**
The principal advantage is that the presence of their relics and images excites us to imitate their virtues.

The Second Commandment of God

135. **Say the second commandment.**
"Thou shalt not take the name of the Lord thy God in vain."[4]

136. **What are we forbidden by the second commandment?**
We are forbidden to make rash, unjust, or false oaths.

137. **What is an oath?**
An oath is an act of religion, by which God is called to witness the truth of what is affirmed or promised.

138. **When is an oath rash?**
An oath is rash when made lightly, without necessity, and for things of little importance.

[4] Ex 20:7

* 139. **What precaution should we take against swearing rashly?**
Never to swear, but when required by a lawful superior.

140. **When is an oath unjust?**
An oath is unjust when it is taken to do an unlawful thing.

141. **Is he who binds himself by an oath to steal, to kill, or to beat another obliged to keep his oath?**
No, by no means; he would commit a new sin by accomplishing it.

142. **When is an oath false?**
An oath is false when the person who takes it knows it to be contrary to truth; and this is what is called a false oath or perjury.

* 143. **Is a false oath a great sin?**
Yes; it is an enormous crime.

144. **What is blasphemy?**
An injurious word against God, or the saints, or against holy things.

145. **Is it a grievous sin to pronounce certain words known in vulgar language by the name of oaths?**
Many of these oaths are but indecent words; many are criminal, and border upon blasphemy; all may become scandalous owing to circumstances; wherefore all good Christians should abstain from uttering them.

146. **What is a vow?**
A vow is a promise made to God, to honor him or his saints, by some pious action.

* 147. **Are we obliged to accomplish our vows?**
Yes, otherwise we should sin.

* 148. **What precaution should we take to avoid making vows rashly?**
Never to make any without consulting our confessor.

The Third Commandment of God

149. **Say the third commandment.**
"Remember to keep holy the sabbath day."[5]

150. **To what are we obliged by the third commandment?**
To sanctify the Sundays by prayer, good works, and holy repose.

The Fourth Commandment of God

151. **Say the fourth commandment.**
"Honor thy father and thy mother."[6]

152. **What are we obliged to by the fourth commandment?**
We are commanded thereby to honor our superiors, particularly our father and mother.

153. **In what does the honor we owe to our father and mother consist?**
It consists in loving, respecting, obeying, and assisting them in their necessities.

154. **Is there any blessing attached to the accomplishment of this precept?**
Yes, God has attached a particular blessing to the children who honor their father and mother.

155. **Are we obliged to honor the king, and to accomplish in temporal matters his orders or those of his representatives?**
Yes; and this obligation is a part of Christian morality.

[5] Ex 20:8
[6] Ex 20:12

156. **What do we owe to our ecclesiastical superiors?**
We owe them respect, love, and obedience in what concerns religion and salvation.

The Fifth Commandment of God

157. **Say the fifth commandment.**
"Thou shalt not kill."[7]

158. **What is forbidden by the fifth commandment?**
We are forbidden to kill, beat, ill treat, or scandalize our neighbor, or, even to have the intention of so doing.

159. **What is meant by "giving scandal to our neighbor"?**
The drawing of him into evil, or the hindering of him from doing good.

The Sixth Commandment of God

160. **Say the sixth commandment.**
"Thou shalt not commit adultery."[8]

161. **What are we forbidden by the sixth commandment?**
All kinds of lewdness and immodesty with oneself or others.

The Seventh Commandment of God

162. **Say the seventh commandment.**
"Thou shalt not steal."[9]

[7] Ex 20:13
[8] Ex 20:14
[9] Ex 20:15

163. **What is forbidden by the seventh commandment?**
To take away, or retain unjustly the goods of our neighbor; or to do him any injustice.

164. **What is he obliged to who has caused any damage to his neighbor?**
He is obliged to make restitution.

The Eighth Commandment of God

165. **Say the eighth commandment.**
"Thou shalt not bear false witness against thy neighbor."[10]

166. **What is forbidden by the eighth commandment?**
It is forbidden to lie, to bear false witness against our neighbor, to judge rashly, to insult or defame him by slander or calumny.

The Ninth Commandment of God

167. **Say the ninth commandment.**
"Thou shalt not covet thy neighbor's wife."[11]

168. **What is forbidden by the ninth commandment?**
To consent to any unchaste thoughts or lustful desires of the flesh.

The Tenth Commandment of God

169. **Say the tenth commandment.**
"Thou shalt not covet thy neighbor's goods."[12]

170. **What is forbidden by the tenth commandment?**
All desires of our neighbor's goods.

[10] Ex 20:16
[11] Ex 20:17
[12] Ibid.

171. **Who are they that are most exposed to transgress the tenth commandment?**
They who are jealous of the credit and prosperity of others.

OF THE COMMANDMENTS OF THE CHURCH

172. **Are all Christians obliged to observe the commandments of the Church?**
Yes; because Christ declares that he that will not hear the Church is to be considered as a heathen and a publican.

173. **Who made the commandments of the Church?**
The body of the chief pastors.

* 174. **How many principal commandments of the Church are there?**
There are seven.[13]

The First Commandment of the Church

175. **Say the first commandment of the Church.**
To keep holy all festivals of obligation.

176. **What is enjoined us by the first commandment of the Church?**
We are bound to sanctify the feasts of obligation, in the same manner as we are obliged to sanctify the Sundays.

The Second Commandment of the Church

177. **Say the second commandment of the Church.**
To hear Mass on Sundays and holy days.

178. **What is commanded by the second commandment of the Church?**
To assist on Sundays and holy days of obligation at Mass, and particularly at the parochial Mass.

[13] See p. 54, above.

The Third Commandment of the Church

179. **Say the third commandment of the Church.**
To confess our sins at least once a year.

180. **What is commanded by the third precept of the Church?**
By this precept, all the faithful, when arrived at the age of discretion, are bound to confess their sins at least once a year.

The Fourth Commandment of the Church

181. **Say the fourth commandment of the Church.**
Worthily to receive the Holy Eucharist about Easter.

182. **What is commanded by the fourth precept of the Church?**
1) To receive the Blessed Eucharist at least once a year, with suitable dispositions. 2) To receive it between Palm Sunday and Low Sunday, and in one's own parish church.

The Fifth Commandment of the Church

183. **Say the fifth commandment of the Church.**
To fast Lent, Ember days, and vigils commanded.

184. **What are we commanded by the fifth commandment of the Church?**
To fast: three days in each Ember week; on the eve of certain festivals; and every day during Lent, except Sundays.

The Sixth Commandment of the Church

185. **Say the sixth commandment of the Church.**
To abstain from flesh meat on Fridays and Saturdays.

186. **What is commanded by the sixth commandment of the Church?**
To abstain from flesh meat: on all the Fridays and Saturdays throughout the year, on the Sundays in Lent, on Saint Mark's day, and on the three Rogation days.

187. **Is it as obligatory to abstain from flesh meat on Saturdays as on Fridays?**
Yes; except the Saturdays between Christmas and Candlemas, when the use of flesh meat is permitted.

188. **Has not the solemnity of Christmas some privilege in this respect?**
Yes; it is always lawful to use flesh meat on Christmas day, even when this festival falls upon Friday or Saturday.

189. **Is abstinence from flesh meat commanded on fast days?**
Yes, always.

190. **What are we to think of those who seldom or never fast; who use flesh meat in Lent, and on Saturdays throughout the year?**
We are to presume that they act from reasons of health or poverty; and that they have consulted their pastors on this head; otherwise, they would be very guilty.

The Seventh Commandment of the Church

191. **Say the seventh commandment of the Church.**
To pay tithes to our pastors.

192. **What is the meaning of the seventh commandment of the Church?**
That the faithful are obliged to pay tithes, offerings, and other authorized dues to defray the expenses of divine worship, and to maintain their pastors.

* 193. **Do the commandments of the Church oblige under pain of mortal sin?**
Yes; and this ought to strike terror into the hearts of all those Christians who observe them ill.

On Prayers

194. **Do we stand in need of any assistance to observe the commandments?**
Yes; we stand in need of the grace of God.

195. **How may we obtain the grace of God?**
By prayer.

* 196. **What is prayer?**
Prayer is an elevation of our heart and mind to God, to render to him our homage and to beg him that of which we stand in need.

* 197. **Do we really pray when we recite a form of prayer without attention and devotion?**
No; because then neither the heart, nor the mind is elevated to God, nor do we ask anything of him.

THE LORD'S PRAYER

* 198. **Which is the most excellent of all prayers?**
The *Pater Noster*, or the Lord's Prayer, taught us by Christ himself.

199. **Say the Lord's Prayer.**
In English:
Our Father who art in heaven.
1. Hallowed be thy name.

2. Thy kingdom come.
3. Thy will be done on earth, as it is in heaven.
4. Give us this day our daily bread.
5. And forgive us our trespasses, as we forgive them that trespass against us.
6. And lead us not into temptation.
7. But deliver us from evil. Amen.

In Latin:

Pater Noster qui es in coelis.

1. *Sanctificetur nomen tuum.*
2. *Adveniat regnum tuum.*
3. *Fiat voluntas tua, sicut in coelo et in terra.*
4. *Panem nostrum quotidianum da nobis hodie.*
5. *Et dimitte nobis debita nostra, sicut et nos dimittimus debitoribus nostris.*
6. *Et ne nos inducas in tentationem.*
7. *Sed libera nos a malo. Amen.*

200. **To whom do we speak when we say, "Our Father"?**
To God.

201. **Why do we call God, "Our Father"?**
Because he is the Creator of all things, the Father of all men, and particularly of good Christians.

202. **Why do we add, "who art in heaven," whereas God is everywhere?**
Because we consider heaven to be, in a particular manner, the throne of his glory.

The First Petition

203. **What do we ask of God, when we say: "Hallowed be thy name"?**
By this, we beg that God may be known, served, and adored by all men, and that his name may be always pronounced with the greatest respect.

The Second Petition

204. **What do we ask of God in this petition: "Thy kingdom come"?**
In this petition, we beg that God may reign in our hearts in this life by his grace, and we with him forever in heaven.

The Third Petition

205. **What do we ask by these words: "Thy will be done on earth as it is in heaven"?**
By this, we beg that God would grant us grace to obey him here on earth, as the saints and angels do in heaven.

The Fourth Petition

206. **What do we ask when we say: "Give us this day our daily bread"?**
By this petition, we beg of God to supply our wants of each day, both for soul and body.

The Fifth Petition

207. **What do we ask by these words: "And forgive us our trespasses"?**
We beg of God that he would be pleased to grant us pardon of all our sins.

208. **Why do you add: "As we forgive them that trespass against us"?**
We thereby consent that God would refuse to pardon us if we do not pardon others the injuries they may have done us.

The Sixth Petition

209. **What do we ask by this petition: "And lead us not into temptation"?**
By this, we beg of God to preserve us from temptations, or give us strength to overcome them.

The Seventh Petition

210. **What do we beg, in fine, by these words: "But deliver us from evil"?**
We pray that God would deliver us from all evil, and particularly from that of sin and eternal death.

THE ANGELICAL SALUTATION

211. **Why do we so often pray to the Blessed Virgin?**
Because she is the most powerful protectress we have in heaven.

212. **Should we have as much confidence in her as in Christ?**
No; because Christ is God, while the Blessed Virgin is but a mere creature.

213. **Does she offer our prayers to God through herself?**
No; she can only offer them through Christ who only is the mediator between God and man.

214. **By what prayer does the Church ordinarily invoke the Blessed Virgin?**
By the Angelical Salutation, called also the *Ave Maria*, or "Hail Mary."

* 215. **Say the Angelical Salutation.**
In English:
Hail Mary, full of grace, the Lord is with thee: blessed art thou amongst women, and blessed is the fruit of thy womb, Jesus.

Holy Mary, Mother of God, pray for us sinners, now and at the hour of our death. Amen.

In Latin:
Ave Maria, gratia plena, Dominus tecum: benedicta tu in mulieribus, et benedictus fructus ventris tui, Jesus.

Sancta Maria, Mater Dei, ora pro nobis peccatoribus, nunc et in hora mortis nostrae. Amen.

216. **How many parts are there in the Angelical Salutation?**
Three.

217. **Which is the first part of the Angelical Salutation?**
The words by which the angel Gabriel announced to the Blessed Virgin Mary the mystery of the incarnation: "Hail, full of grace, the Lord is with thee."[14]

218. **Which is the second part of the Angelical Salutation?**
The words spoken by St. Elizabeth, when visited by the Blessed Virgin: "Blessed art thou among women, and blessed is the fruit of thy womb, Jesus."[15]

219. **Which is the third part of the Angelical Salutation?**
The words added by the piety of the faithful and approved by the Church: "Holy Mary, Mother of God, pray for us sinners, now and at the hour of our death."

220. **Why do you call the Virgin Mary, "Mother of God"?**
Because she conceived and brought forth Christ, the Son of God and second Person of the Holy Trinity.

THE ROSARY

221. **What is the rosary?**
The rosary, or psalter of the Blessed Virgin, is a prayer chiefly composed of 150 Hail Marys.

222. **How is the rosary divided?**
Into fifteen parts.

[14] Lk 1:28
[15] Cf. Lk 1:42

223. **What does each part contain?**
One *Pater Noster* or Our Father, with ten *Ave Marias* or Hail Marys, to which is added the *Gloria Patri* or "Glory be to the Father," etc.

224. **What is the chaplet or beads of the Blessed Virgin?**
It is the third part of the rosary, or fifty Hail Marys.

225. **How do you commence the chaplet?**
By the sign of the cross, the Creed or "I believe in God," three Hail Marys, and the *Gloria Patri.*

226. **Why these three Hail Marys?**
To honor the relation of the Holy Virgin with the three Persons of the Blessed Trinity.

227. **Is there any virtue in the number of Our Fathers, Hail Marys, or *Gloria Patris* which constitute the beads?**
No; the beads derives all its virtue from excellent prayers which it contains, and from the spirit of fervor with which it is recited.

228. **Is it not useless so often to recite the same prayers?**
No; provided the heart join with the lips.

229. **What particular advantage is found in the beads?**
It is of great service to those who cannot read.

230. **How is the beads concluded?**
By the prayer, *Sub tuum praesidium* or "We fly to thy patronage," etc.[16]

[16] See p. 54, above.

Exercises of a Christian Life

DAILY EXERCISES

231. **What should a Christian do every day of his life?**

If he wishes to lead a holy life, he must every day:

1. On awaking in the morning, make upon himself the sign of the cross and say, "O my God, I offer thee my heart."
2. Having clothed himself modestly, he should kneel down and say his morning prayers.
3. Hear Mass, if he can conveniently.
4. Apply himself to the affairs of his calling.
5. Take his meals with sobriety and temperance, saying grace, before and after meat.[17]
6. Help the poor according to his means.
7. Examine his conscience and say evening prayers at a proper hour, and, as much as possible, with the whole family.

232. **How ought he to sanctify his actions?**

By offering them up to God.

233. **What is he to do in the troubles and contradictions of life?**

He should suffer them with patience in atonement for his sins, and unite them with the sufferings of Christ.

234. **What should he do in the time of temptation?**

Recommend himself to God, and avoid such discourses and objects as may entice him to evil.

[17] See p. 55, above.

235. **If he fears that he has fallen into mortal sins, what should he do?**
Humble himself immediately, beg pardon of God, and go to confession as soon as possible.

236. **What conduct should he pursue with respect to amusements?**
Not to indulge more in them than they are necessary and innocent.

EXERCISES FOR PARTICULAR TIMES

237. **What ought a Christian to do on Sundays and holy days?**
He ought to abstain from all servile works, from amusements, from journeys on account of his temporal affairs; and to assist at the parish Mass, at vespers, and at the Christian instructions given on those days.

238. **What is it expedient for him to do every month?**
To confess his sins, and receive the Holy Communion according to the advice of his confessor.

239. **What should he do on every year?**
To review his conscience, in order to prepare for the paschal or Easter Communion.

240. **How should we conduct ourselves during the time of sickness?**
We should receive our sickness with resignation to the will of God; and if it be dangerous, prepare ourselves religiously for death.

241. **What should we do when one of our friends or relations is dangerously ill?**
We should exhort him to settle his temporal affairs, send for a priest, and receive the last sacraments.

Of the Sacraments

* 242. **What is a sacrament?**
A sacrament is a sensible or outward sign instituted by our Lord Jesus Christ in order to sanctify us.

243. **Why do you say that a sacrament is a "sensible sign"?**
It is a sign, because it signifies the grace it produces in us; and it is sensible or outward, because it is perceptible to our senses.

* 244. **How many sacraments has Jesus Christ instituted?**
Seven: baptism, confirmation, Eucharist, penance, extreme unction, holy orders, and matrimony.

245. **Can we receive the same sacraments more than once?**
Yes; all except baptism, confirmation, and holy orders.

* 246. **Which are the sacraments that must be received in the state of grace?**
All except baptism and penance.

* 247. **What would be the consequence if we received the other sacraments in the state of mortal sin?**
We would commit as many sacrileges.

248. **What is a sacrilege?**
The profanation of a holy thing; and the more holy the thing is, the greater is the sacrilege.

OF BAPTISM

* 249. **What is baptism?**

Baptism is a sacrament which takes away original sin and makes us Christians and children of God and of his Church.

250. **Can all persons baptize?**

Yes; in the case of absolute necessity.

* 251. **How is baptism given?**

By pouring water on the head of the person to be baptized, saying at the same time: "I baptize thee in the name of the Father, and of the Son, and of the Holy Ghost."

OF CONFIRMATION

* 252. **What is confirmation?**

Confirmation is a sacrament which imparts the Holy Ghost, with the abundance of his graces.

* 253. **Who is the Holy Ghost?**

The third Person of the Holy Trinity.[18]

* 254. **Why is the Holy Ghost imparted to us in the sacrament of confirmation?**

To make us perfect Christians.

* 255. **How does confirmation make us perfect Christians?**

By giving us strength to confess Christ.

* 256. **In what does the confessing of Christ consist?**

In openly declaring for him, and for the maxims of his holy law.

[18] The rest of this article is only proper for persons about to receive the sacrament of confirmation.

* 257. **Does Christ require of us to declare for him in this manner?**
Yes; for he says in the gospel that, at the day of judgment, he will acknowledge before his heavenly Father all those who shall have acknowledged him before men; but that he will deny those who shall have denied him and his doctrine.

258. **By whom is the sacrament of confirmation administered?**
By the bishop.

259. **What ceremonies are used in the administration of this sacrament?**
The bishop prays for those he confirms, lays his hands on them, and anoints their foreheads with holy chrism in the form of a cross.

260. **What does the laying on of the bishop's hands signify?**
It signifies that the Holy Ghost comes to reside in the souls of those who receive this sacrament with suitable dispositions.

261. **What is holy chrism?**
Holy chrism is a composition of oil and balm, consecrated by the bishop on Maundy or Holy Thursday.

262. **Are there not other ceremonies used in the administration of this sacrament?**
Yes; the bishop gives the person he confirms a slight stroke on the cheek, saying: "Peace be with thee."

263. **Why does he do so?**
To put us in mind that, after the example of Christ, we should patiently endure all sorts of injuries.

* 264. **What are the necessary qualifications for the reception of this sacrament?**
We should have: 1) a sufficient knowledge of the mysteries of religion; 2) be in the state of sanctifying grace; and 3) have a great desire to receive the Holy Ghost.

265. **Would it be a sin not to receive the sacrament of confirmation?**
Yes; if it were through neglect, contempt, or any attachment to sin.

* 266. **Is there any particular motive that should induce us to receive the sacrament of confirmation worthily?**
Yes; and this motive is: because we can receive it but once.

OF THE EUCHARIST[19]

Of the Eucharist in General

* 267. **What is the Eucharist?**
The Eucharist is a sacrament that contains really and truly the body and blood, soul and divinity of our Lord Jesus Christ, under the forms of bread and wine.

* 268. **How does the sacrament of the Eucharist become the body and blood of Christ?**
By the words of consecration, which the priest pronounces.

* 269. **What is the effect of those words?**
By the words of consecration, the bread is changed into the true body, and the wine into the true blood of Christ.

270. **How is the change called?**
It is called transubstantiation, that is, the change of one substance into another.

* 271. **Does anything of the bread and wine remain after the consecration?**
No; there remains nothing but the forms and appearances.

[19] The Eucharist is placed here to observe the order of the sacraments; but full liberty is left to those catechists who would rather have it placed after the sacrament of penance.

272. **What do you mean by "the forms or appearances"?**
I mean thereby what falls under our senses, as the figure, color, taste, etc.

* 273. **Is there anything but the body of Jesus Christ under the form of bread?**
There is also his blood, together with his soul and divinity; in a word, the whole Person of Jesus Christ.

* 274. **And under the form of wine?**
The whole Person of Jesus Christ is there likewise.

* 275. **When the host is divided, under what part is Christ?**
He is whole and entire under each part.

276. **When a part only of the host, or one form, is received, is Christ received wholly?**
Yes; because Christ is whole under each form, and under each part of the forms.

* 277. **Should we adore the body and blood of Christ in the Eucharist?**
Yes; by all means; because the body and blood of Jesus Christ are inseparably united to his divinity.

Of the Mass

* 278. **Where is the sacrament of the Eucharist operated?**
At the Holy Mass.

* 279. **What is the Mass?**
The Mass is the oblation of the body and blood of Christ, made to God by the priest.

280. **What should principally occupy us during the Mass?**
We should offer Christ to the Holy Trinity, with the same intentions as he offers himself.

281. **Which are those intentions?**

They are: 1) to adore God; 2) to appease his wrath; 3) to implore his graces; 4) to thank him for all his benefits and blessings.

282. **How may we assist profitably at Mass, by the help of these four points?**

1) From the beginning of the Mass to the gospel, by adoring God, and acknowledging our nothingness before him. 2) From the gospel to the elevation, by appeasing his wrath by humbling ourselves on account of our sins. 3) From the elevation to the communion, by praying for the help of divine grace. 4) From the communion to the end of the Mass, by returning thanks for all the blessings we have received. This method of hearing Mass is particularly recommended to such as cannot read.

Of Communion

* 283. **What is meant by *Communion*?**

The receiving of the sacrament of the Eucharist.

284. **When are we obliged to receive the Communion?**

On three principal occasions: 1) when we have attained the age of discretion, and are sufficiently prepared, in the opinion of our pastors; 2) every year at Easter, according to the fourth commandment of the Church; 3) when we are in danger of death.

* 285. **What dispositions of the soul should accompany us to the Holy Communion?**

The first disposition is to be in the state of grace; the second is to have a great desire of receiving our Lord Jesus Christ.

* 286. **What is understood by being in the state of grace?**

Not to have our conscience burthened with any mortal sin.

* 287. **If we received the Blessed Eucharist in the state of mortal sin, would we really receive Jesus Christ?**

Yes; but we would profane his body and blood.

288. **What dispositions of the body should we bring to the Holy Communion?**

1) We should be decently and modestly dressed; 2) we should neither have eaten nor drunk from midnight, unless we are to receive the Blessed Sacrament by way of viaticum.

289. **May we receive the Blessed Eucharist at any other time than at Mass?**

We should not, without some reason.

290. **How should we occupy ourselves during the Mass, at which we are to receive?**

We should occupy ourselves with the pious sentiments expressed in the following prayer, which may be repeated several times by those who cannot read.

* *Prayer before Communion.*—"Divine Jesus! although thou art not visible to the eyes of my body, I believe that it is thyself, whom thou art about to give me. Alas! I am very unworthy of so great a favor, after having dishonored thee so often; but thy infinite goodness overcomes my rebellious heart, makes me weep over my sins, and fills me with love for thee, and with the most ardent desire of receiving thee. Come then, Savior of the world, purify me from all its stains, and establish thy throne therein forever."

291. **What is to be done after Communion?**

A quarter of an hour at least should be spent in returning thanks to God, for having given himself to us.

292. **How should we conclude this thanksgiving?**

By an entire oblation of ourselves to our Lord. They, who cannot read, may make use of the following prayer.

* *Prayer after Communion.*—"It is true, O Redeemer of mankind, that thou dwellest within me, and that I am in possession of thy body and

blood, soul and divinity. Accept, O Lord, my most profound adoration, which I unite with those that the angels and saints render thee in heaven. O! what love, what gratitude can ever equal the favor which thou hast bestowed on me! Accept, divine Jesus, the offering of all I have, and of all I am: dispose thereof according to thy good pleasure, and grant me grace never to offend thee more."

293. **What are we to think of those who go out of the church immediately after having received the Holy Communion, without having performed this duty?**
We are to suppose that they are sick, or called away by some urgent duty of religion or charity; otherwise, they would be guilty of a great irreverence.

294. **How should we pass the day on which we have had the happiness of receiving?**
We should pass it in retirement; frequently raise up our hearts to God; pay, if possible, a visit to the Blessed Sacrament in the afternoon, and remember, with gratitude and love, the favor received on that day.

OF PENANCE

* 295. **What is penance?**
Penance is a sacrament which remits the sins committed after baptism.

* 296. **Where is the sacrament of penance received?**
It is received in the place where we confess, that is to say, commonly at the confessional.

297. **What are we to do in order worthily to receive the sacrament of penance?**
We should confess all our sins with sorrow to an approved priest; and beg pardon of God, with the resolution of satisfying.

Of Absolution

* 298. **Do we receive the sacrament of penance as often as we go to confession?**
No; we only receive it when the priest gives us absolution.

* 299. **What is absolution?**
The pardon of sins granted by the priest, in the name of Christ.

300. **Does not the priest grant us pardon of our sins every time we go to confession?**
No; sometimes he thinks it necessary to defer absolution, in order to be the better assured of the dispositions of the penitent.

301. **What should a penitent do when the confessor withholds absolution?**
He should submit to that delay with humility, remove the cause thereof, and prepare himself better for another time.

Of Confession

* 302. **What is confession?**
Confession is the declaration of our sins made to the priest in order to receive absolution.

303. **What qualities should this declaration have?**
It should be humble, sincere, and entire.

304. **In what does the humility of confession consist?**
In declaring our sins with great confusion for having offended God.

305. **In what does the sincerity of confession consist?**
In declaring our sins candidly as they are known to us, without exaggeration or excuse.

306. **In what does the integrity of confession consist?**
In declaring all the mortal sins we may have committed, as far as we can remember them, after a serious examination.

307. **Should we also declare the number of times we may have committed each sin?**
Yes.

308. **Would it not be enough to say, "I have committed this sin often, sometimes, many times," etc.?**
No; this would not be an entire confession.

309. **Must we also declare the circumstances of our sins?**
Yes; when they change the nature of the sin, or notably aggravate the malice thereof.

310. **Give an example of a circumstance that changes the species of sin?**
The stealing of a holy vessel is not only a theft, but likewise a sacrilege.

311. **Give an example of a circumstance which notably aggravates the malice of sin?**
To speak ill of my neighbor from a motive of revenge; the sin is greater than to speak ill of him merely for the sake of talking.

* 312. **Would it be a great evil to conceal in confession a mortal sin, or some mortal circumstance of a sin?**
Yes; it would render the confession null and sacrilegious.

* 313. **What is he obliged to do who has made such a confession?**
To recommence it, and to accuse himself particularly of the crime committed, by concealing such a sin, or such a circumstance.

314. **Would we become guilty, if through a negligent examination of our conscience, a mortal sin, or some notable circumstance were forgotten?**
Yes; we would become guilty.

Of Examination of Conscience

315. **How should we prepare to examine our conscience?**

By the sentiments expressed in the following prayer, composed for those persons who cannot read.

* *Prayer before the examination of conscience.*—"Behold me, O Lord! at thy feet, in order to declare unto thee, in the person of thy minister, all the sins of which I am guilty. Grant me grace to know them, and to confess them all with sincerity, and to detest them with all my heart. Amen."

* 316. **How are we to examine our conscience?**

By bringing to mind our thoughts, words, actions, and omissions.

* 317. **How may we know whether we have offended God by our thoughts, words, actions, or omissions?**

By comparing them with the commandments of God and of the Church.

318. **Give me an instance of this.**

By despising my parents, I sin in thought against the fourth commandment of God; by holding indecent conversation, I sin in words against the sixth commandment; by taking what belongs to another person, I sin by action against the seventh commandment; by not hearing Mass on a holy day of obligation, I sin by omission against the second commandment of the Church.

319. **Should we examine our conscience on any other points?**

Yes; it is proper to examine our conscience on the capital sins, on our habits and passions, on the duties of our calling, and on the places and persons we have frequented.

320. **What length of time should we employ in the examination of our conscience before confession?**

As much as we would reasonably employ in preparing for an important affair.

321. **How should we finish the examination of conscience?**
By an act of contrition.

322. **Make an act of contrition.**
"O my God, I am heartily sorry for having offended thee, because thou art infinitely good and infinitely amiable, because sin is displeasing to thee; pardon me through the merits of Jesus Christ my Savior; I propose, with the help of thy holy grace, never more to offend thee, and to do penance."

Of Contrition

* 323. **In order to obtain pardon in the sacrament of penance, is it sufficient to declare our sins to the priest?**
No; we must moreover indispensably have contrition.

* 324. **What is contrition?**
Sorrow and regret for having offended God, with a firm resolution never-more to offend him.

325. **Is it enough to repeat one or more acts of contrition, in order to believe that we have this sorrow?**
No; contrition must proceed from the heart, for it must be interior.

326. **Can we of ourselves produce that sorrow in our heart?**
No; it is a gift of God, which we must humbly beg of him, and which can come from no other source.

327. **Would that contrition be sufficient which proceeds from a sorrow for having offended God, on account of the dishonor, or temporal loss which ensues?**
No; it would be merely a worldly sorrow; whereas the contrition which procures the pardon of sin ought to be supernatural.

328. **On what motives ought our contrition to be grounded?**
On the following: 1) the infinite goodness of God whom we have offended; 2) the benefits of God, and our own ingratitude; 3) the passion and death of Jesus Christ, of which our sins are the cause; 4) hell that we have merited, and heaven that we have lost.

329. **Should our sorrow for having offended God be very great?**
Sin being the greatest of all evils, our sorrow for having committed it should be the greatest of all sorrows, and this is the reason why contrition ought to be sovereign.

* 330. **Is it enough to detest only a part of our mortal sins?**
No; because contrition ought to be universal.

* 331. **May we limit the resolution of not offending God to some days or months?**
No; we must be resolved never more to offend him.

Exercise of Confession

* 332. **When the time of confession is come, what are we to do?**
To kneel down by the confessor, so as not to look at him in the face, make the sign of the cross, and say:

In English: "Bless me, Father, for I have sinned. I confess to Almighty God," etc.—as far as "through my fault."[20]

In Latin: *Benedic mihi, Pater, quia peccavi. Confiteor Deo omnipotenti,* etc.—as far as, *mea culpa.*[21]

* 333. **What are we afterwards to do?**
We must declare how long it is since we were at confession last; whether we received absolution; and whether we have performed the penance

[20] See p. 51, above.
[21] Ibid.

imposed on us. Then we commence our confession, saying at each article, "I accuse myself of...," etc.

* 334. **The accusation of sins being ended, what are we to say?**
We should say: "I accuse myself moreover of many other sins which I do not, at this present time, remember, and of those of my whole life; for which I beg pardon of God, and of you, my ghostly Father, penance and absolution."

335. **How should we receive the admonitions of our confessor?**
We should receive them with much respect, and with a desire to reduce them to practice; with submission to the penance he imposes; and then finish the *confiteor*.

In English: "Through my fault," etc.

In Latin: *Mea culpa*, etc.

336. **If the confessor thinks proper to grant us absolution, what are we to do?**
While he is giving it, we should renew our act of contrition, then retire; thank God for the grace just received, and perform, as soon as possible, the penance enjoined.

337. **In what terms should we express to God our thankfulness for having received absolution?**
They who cannot read may say the following prayer, as often as they choose.

* *Prayer after confession.*—"I am no longer thy enemy, O my God! By the virtue of the sacrament which I have just received, thou hast healed the wounds of my soul; thou hast received me into thy favor; thou hast revived the merits of my good works, which were dead through sin, and thou hast changed in a temporal punishment the eternal damnation which my sins deserved. Grant me, O God, the gift of perseverance in thy service. Ah! rather let me die a thousand deaths than offend thee again."

Of Satisfaction

* 338. **What is satisfaction?**

It is a reparation we owe to God and our neighbor for the injury or wrong done them by sin.

339. **How can we satisfy God?**

We satisfy God: 1) by the pains and afflictions of this life, when we accept them with patience and resignation; 2) by the performance of satisfactory works, as prayers, fasting, and alms; 3) and principally, by the faithful accomplishment of the penance enjoined by the confessor.

340. **Can we of ourselves satisfy the divine justice?**

No; Christ only, our sovereign mediator, can render our satisfactions meritorious by offering them to God his Father.

341. **How can we satisfy our neighbor?**

By repairing the wrong done him in his person, his goods, or his honor.

342. **What do you mean by *indulgences*?**

By *indulgences* we mean the remission, granted by the Church, of the temporal punishment due to sin after the guilt is remitted.

343. **What are we to do in order to obtain an indulgence?**

We must be in a state of grace, and faithfully accomplish the conditions on which it is granted by the pope or by the bishop.

OF EXTREME UNCTION

* 344. **What is extreme unction?**

Extreme unction is a sacrament instituted by Jesus Christ for the spiritual and bodily ease of the sick.

345. **At what time is this sacrament to be received?**
When we are in danger of death by sickness; but we should not wait till the last moment.

OF HOLY ORDERS

* 346. **What is understood by "holy orders"?**
Holy orders is a sacrament which gives power to perform the clerical functions, and grace to perform them worthily.

OF MATRIMONY

* 347. **What is matrimony?**
Matrimony is a sacrament which sanctifies the union of the married couple.

348. **To what are they exposed who receive the sacrament of marriage in the state of mortal sin?**
Besides the sacrilegious profanation of this sacrament, of which they become guilty, they expose themselves and their children to incur the malediction of God.

Festivals of Obligation

Throughout the Diocese of Quebec

All Sundays of the year.
The Circumcision of Our Lord, Jan. 1st.
The Epiphany of Our Lord, Jan. 6th.

The Annunciation of the Blessed Virgin Mary, March 25th.[22]
The Ascension of Our Lord.
Corpus Christi day.
Sts. Peter and Paul, June 29th.
All Saints' day, Nov. 1st.
The Conception of the Blessed Virgin Mary, Dec. 8th.
Christmas day, Dec. 25th.

Festivals of Devotion

Monday and Tuesday in Easter week.
Monday and Tuesday in Whitsunday week.
The eighth day after Corpus Christi day.
The festival of St. Stephen, First Martyr, Dec. 26th.
The festival of St. John, Apostle, Dec. 27th.

Solemnities Transferred to Sundays

The first Sunday in the month of February.—The Purification of the Blessed Virgin Mary.
The first Sunday after the 19th of February.—St. Matthias.
The first Sunday after the 13th of March.—St. Joseph, First Patron of the Country.
The first Sunday after the 29th of April.—Sts. Philip and James.
The first Sunday after the 20th of June.—St. John the Baptist.
The first Sunday after the 18th of July.—St. James.
The first Sunday after the 25th of July.—St. Ann.
The first Sunday after the 6th of August.—St. Lawrence.
The first Sunday after the 15th of August.—St. Bartholomew.
The first Sunday after the 24th of August.—St. Lewis.
The first Sunday after the 6th of September.—The Nativity of the Blessed Virgin Mary.

[22] When the festival of the Annunciation is transferred to another day than the 25th of March, it ceases to be of obligation.

The first Sunday after the 16th of September.—St. Matthew.
The first Sunday after the 23rd of September.—St. Michael.
The first Sunday after the 24th of October.—St. Simon and St. Jude.
The last Sunday in the month of November.—St. Andrew.
The Sunday before the Conception.—St. Francis Xavier, Second Patron of the Country.
The Sunday before Christmas day.—St. Thomas.

Particular Festivals Falling on the Sundays

The Second Sunday after the Epiphany.—The Holy Name of Jesus.
The Third Sunday after Easter.—The Holy Family of Jesus, Mary, Joseph.
The second Sunday in the month of July.—The Dedication of the cathedral church and other churches of the diocese.
The first Sunday after the 14th of August.—The Assumption of the Blessed Virgin Mary.
The first Sunday in the month of October.—The Holy Rosary.
The nearest Sunday to the 22nd of October.—The festival of Our Lady of Victory.
The first Sunday after All Saints' day.—The patronal festivals of the parishes.

Fast Days

1. Every day in Lent, except Sundays.
2. The Ember days, or the Wednesdays, Fridays, and Saturdays immediately following:
    the First Sunday of Lent;
    Whitsunday;
    the 14th of September, or the Exaltation of the Holy Cross;
    and the 13th of December, or the Third Sunday of Advent.
3. The following eves or vigils:
    of Christmas day;
    of Whitsunday;

of St. John the Baptist;
of Sts. Peter and Paul;
of St. Lawrence;
of the Assumption of the Blessed Virgin Mary;
of St. Matthew;
of Sts. Simon and Jude;
of All Saints;
of St. Andrew.

Note.—If any of these vigils happen on a Sunday, the fast day is to be kept on the preceding Saturday.

When the solemnity of a festival is transferred to the Sunday, the fast day is kept on the Saturday, the eve of that solemnity.

Days of Abstinence from Flesh Meat, though Not Fasts

1. Every Sunday in Lent.
2. St. Mark's day (25th of April), unless this festival falls in Easter week; for, in this case, both the abstinence and procession to be observed on that day are transferred to the Monday after Low Sunday. But when the 25th of April falls on one of the Sundays after Low Sunday, then there is no abstinence on St Mark's day.
3. Rogation days, or the three days before Ascension.
4. Every Friday throughout the year.
5. Every Saturday, except from Christmas till the solemnity of the Purification.

Note.—If Christmas falls on a Friday or Saturday, flesh meat is allowed on that day.

Advent

The First Sunday of Advent is always the nearest Sunday to St. Andrew's day, either before or after; that is, from the 27th of November to the 3rd of December, inclusively.

Times in Which the Church Forbids the Solemnizing of Marriage

The solemnizing of marriage is forbidden from the First Sunday of Advent till the Epiphany, inclusively, and from Ash Wednesday till Low Sunday, also inclusively. At all other times, it may be solemnized.

The Manner of Lay Persons Baptizing an Infant in Case of Danger of Death

Take common water, pour it on the head of the child, and, when you are pouring it, say the following words: "I baptize thee in the name of the Father, and of the Son, and of the Holy Ghost."

Necessary Rules for a Christian

You must often examine your thoughts, words, and actions, especially after much business, conversation, etc., that you may discern and amend your faults.

Hold your peace in things that do not belong to you, and where your interference will not redound to the honor of God and the good of your neighbor.

Often call to mind your past life, and what our Savior suffered for you every hour of his life.

You must live as though you possessed nothing, and yet possessed all things: and remember, that meat, drink, and clothings are a Christian's riches.

Offer yourself up entirely to God: and though you have nothing wherewith to requite his favors, you will be comforted, when you consider that he gives all, who gives himself.

The apostles left their poor boats and nets, and received in return a most ample reward. The poor widow gave only two mites, and her offering was preferred to those of the richest persons.

He easily parts with all things, who always considers that he must die, and be separated from them.

In public assemblies, use no extravagant or unusual gestures; but in all things, observe great modesty and discretion.

In all things, desire and prefer that which conduceth most to the service and glory of God; such as to comfort the afflicted, reconcile those that are at variance, visit the sick and prisoners, and relieve the poor.

Never go to bed with any uneasiness of mind, but endeavor to pacify your conscience by confession or an act of contrition.

Every month, at least, confess your sins, make frequent acts of contrition, and daily use aspirations or ejaculatory prayers; in order to prevent the deceits of the evil one.

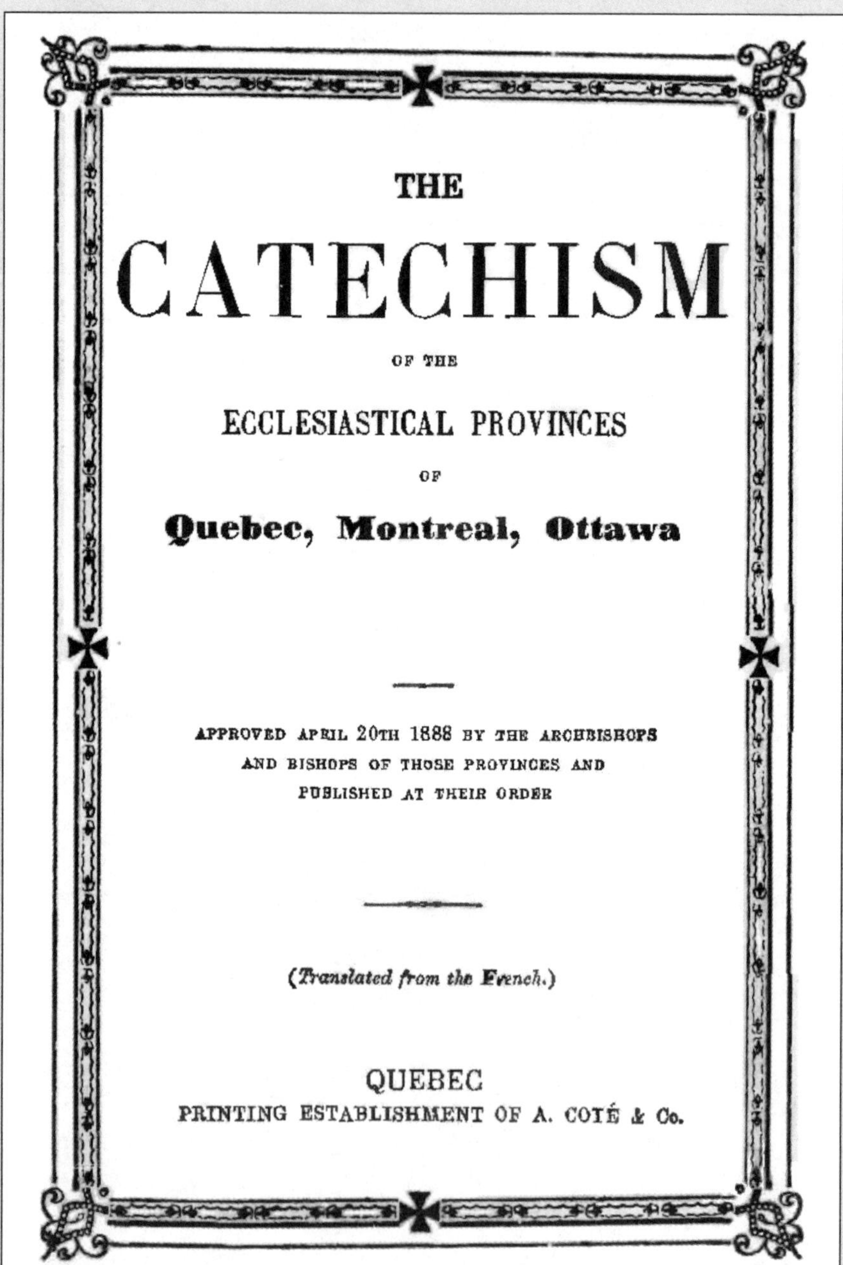

THE

CATECHISM

OF THE

ECCLESIASTICAL PROVINCES

OF

Quebec, Montreal, Ottawa

APPROVED APRIL 20TH 1888 BY THE ARCHBISHOPS
AND BISHOPS OF THOSE PROVINCES AND
PUBLISHED AT THEIR ORDER

(*Translated from the French.*)

QUEBEC
PRINTING ESTABLISHMENT OF A. COTÉ & Co.

Original Title Page

THE

CATECHISM

OF THE

ECCLESIASTICAL PROVINCES

OF

Quebec, Montreal, Ottawa

APPROVED APRIL 20TH 1888 BY THE ARCHBISHOPS
AND BISHOPS OF THOSE PROVINCES AND
PUBLISHED AT THEIR ORDER

(Translated from the French.)

QUEBEC
PRINTING ESTABLISHMENT OF A. COTÉ & Co.

Imprimatur:
Quebeci, die 15a augusti 1888.
E. A. Card. Taschereau,
Archpus Quebecen.

Christian Prayers

To be taught to children, at least in their mother tongue, in order that they may recite them morning and evening.

The Sign of the Cross

+ *In nomine Patris, et Filii, et Spiritus Sancti. Amen.*

+ In the name of the Father, and of the Son, and of the Holy Ghost. Amen.

The Lord's Prayer

Pater noster, qui es in coelis.

1. *Sanctificetur nomen tuum.*
2. *Adveniat regnum tuum.*
3. *Fiat voluntas tua sicut in coelo et in terra.*
4. *Panem nostrum quotidianum da nobis hodie.*
5. *Et dimitte nobis debita nostra, sicut et nos dimittimus debitoribus nostris.*
6. *Et ne nos inducas in tentationem.*
7. *Sed libera nos a malo. Amen.*

Our Father who art in heaven.

1. Hallowed be thy name.
2. Thy kingdom come.
3. Thy will be done on earth as it is in heaven.
4. Give us this day our daily bread.
5. And forgive us our trespasses, as we forgive them who trespass against us.
6. And lead us not into temptation.
7. But deliver us from evil. Amen.

The Angelical Salutation

Ave Maria, gratia plena, Dominus tecum: benedicta tu in mulieribus, et benedictus fructus ventris tui, Jesus.

Sancta Maria, Mater Dei, ora pro nobis peccatoribus, nunc et in hora mortis nostrae. Amen.

Hail Mary, full of grace, the Lord is with thee; blessed art thou amongst women, and blessed is the fruit of thy womb, Jesus.

Holy Mary, Mother of God, pray for us sinners, now and at the hour of our death. Amen.

The Apostles' Creed

1. *Credo in Deum Patrem omnipotentem, Creatorem coeli et terrae.*
2. *Et in Jesum Christum Filium ejus unicum, Dominum nostrum.*
3. *Qui conceptus est de Spiritu Sancto, natus ex Maria Virgine.*
4. *Passus sub Pontio Pilato, crucifixus, mortuus, et sepultus.*
5. *Descendit ad inferos: tertia die resurrexit a mortuis.*
6. *Ascendit ad coelos, sedet ad dexteram Dei Patris omnipotentis.*
7. *Inde venturus est judicare vivos et mortuos.*
8. *Credo in Spiritum Sanctum.*
9. *Sanctam Ecclesiam Catholicam, sanctorum communionem.*
10. *Remissionem peccatorum.*
11. *Carnis resurrectionem.*
12. *Vitam aeternam. Amen.*

1. I believe in God, the Father Almighty, Creator of heaven and earth.
2. And in Jesus Christ, his only Son, our Lord.
3. Who was conceived by the Holy Ghost, born of the Virgin Mary.
4. Suffered under Pontius Pilate, was crucified, died, and was buried.
5. He descended into hell: the third day he arose again from the dead.
6. He ascended into heaven, sitteth at the right hand of God, the Father Almighty.

7. From thence he shall come to judge the living and the dead.
8. I believe in the Holy Ghost.
9. The holy Catholic Church, the communion of saints.
10. The forgiveness of sins.
11. The resurrection of the body.
12. And the life everlasting. Amen.

The Confiteor

Confiteor Deo omnipotenti, Beatae Mariae semper Virgini, beato Michaeli archangelo, beato Joanni Baptistae, sanctis apostolis Petro et Paulo, omnibus sanctis, (et tibi, Pater,) quia peccavi nimis, cogitatione, verbo, et opere, mea culpa, mea culpa, mea maxima culpa. Ideo precor Beatam Mariam semper Virginem, beatum Michaelem archangelum, beatum Joannem Baptistam, sanctos apostolos Petrum et Paulum, omnes sanctos, (et te, Pater,) orare pro me ad Dominum Deum nostrum.

P. *Misereatur nostri omnipotens Deus, et, dimissis peccatis nostris, perducat nos ad vitam aeternam.*

R. *Amen.*

P. *Indulgentiam, absolutionem, et remissionem peccatorum nostrorum, tribuat nobis omnipotens et misericors Dominus.*

R. *Amen.*

I confess to Almighty God, to Blessed Mary ever Virgin, to blessed Michael the archangel, to blessed John the Baptist, to the holy apostles Peter and Paul, to all the saints, (and to you, Father,) that I have sinned exceedingly in thought, word, and deed, through my fault, through my fault, through my most grievous fault. Therefore, I beseech Blessed Mary ever Virgin, blessed Michael the archangel, blessed John the Baptist, the holy apostles Peter and Paul, and all the saints, (and you, Father,) to pray to the Lord our God for me.

P. May the Almighty God be merciful unto you, and, forgiving you your sins, bring you to life everlasting.

R. Amen.

P. May the Almighty and merciful Lord grant us pardon, absolution, and remission of our sins.

R. Amen.

An Act of Adoration

O my God, I adore thee and acknowledge thee to be my Creator, my sovereign Lord, and the absolute master of all things.

An Act of Faith[1]

O my God, I firmly believe all that the holy Catholic Church believes and teaches, because thou hast said it, and because thou art truth itself.

An Act of Hope

O my God, relying on thy promises, and upon the merits of Jesus Christ my Savior, I hope with a firm confidence that thou wilt give me grace to observe thy commandments in this world and to obtain, by this means, life everlasting.

An Act of Love or Charity

O my God, who art worthy of all my love, on account of thy infinite perfections, I love thee with all my heart, and I love my neighbor as myself for the love of thee.

[1] An indulgence of seven years and seven times forty days each time we recite the acts of faith, hope, and charity, and a plenary indulgence once a month, if we have recited these acts during the month, can be gained on the ordinary conditions of confession, Communion, and a prayer according to the intentions of the sovereign pontiff (Benedict XIV, 1756).

An Act of Contrition

O my God, I am heartily sorry for having offended thee, because thou art infinitely good and infinitely amiable, and because sin displeases thee; pardon me through the merits of Jesus Christ my Savior; I purpose, by the help of thy grace, never more to offend thee and to do penance.

An Act of Thanksgiving

O my God, I thank thee for all the gifts I have received from thee, especially for having created me, redeemed me by thy Son, and made me a child of thy Church.

An Act of Offering

O my God, I have received all from thee: I offer thee my thoughts, my words, my actions, my life and possessions, and for thy service alone do I wish to employ them.

An Act of Humility

O my God, I am but dust and ashes; restrain that spirit of pride which arises in my soul, and teach me to despise myself, thou who resisteth the proud and giveth grace to the humble.

An Act of Petition

O my God, infinite source of all benefits, give me whatever is necessary for the life and health of my body, but especially the grace to perform thy holy will in all things. Through Jesus Christ our Lord. Amen.

The Ten Commandments of God

1. I am the Lord thy God, thou shalt not have strange gods before me.
2. Thou shalt not take the name of the Lord thy God in vain.

3. Remember that thou keep holy the sabbath day.
4. Honor thy father and thy mother.
5. Thou shalt not kill.
6. Thou shalt not commit adultery.
7. Thou shalt not steal.
8. Thou shalt not bear false witness against thy neighbor.
9. Thou shalt not covet thy neighbor's wife.
10. Thou shalt not covet thy neighbor's goods.

The Seven Commandments of the Church

1. Thou shalt sanctify the holy days which are commanded thee.
2. Thou shalt hear Mass on Sundays and holy days.
3. Thou shalt confess thy sins at least once a year.
4. Thou shalt humbly receive thy Creator, at least at Easter time.
5. Thou shalt fast on the Ember days, vigils, and throughout Lent.[2]
6. Thou shalt not eat flesh meat on Fridays or Saturdays.[3]
7. Thou shalt faithfully pay to the Church her rights and tithes.

Doxology to the Blessed Trinity

Gloria Patri, et Filio, et Spiritui Sancto.

Sicut erat in principio, et nunc, et semper, et in saecula saeculorum. Amen.

Glory be to the Father, and to the Son, and to the Holy Ghost.

As it was in the beginning, is now, and ever shall be, world without end. Amen.

[2] See below, p. 124 and 126, for what has been regulated concerning us as to these two commandments, according to an indult of July 7, 1844.

[3] Ibid.

A Prayer to the Blessed Virgin

Sub tuum praesidium confugimus, sancta Dei Genitrix; nostras deprecationes ne despicias in necessitatibus; sed a periculis cunctis libera nos semper, Virgo gloriosa et benedicta.

We fly to thy patronage, O holy Mother of God, despise not our petitions in our necessities; but deliver us always from all dangers, O glorious and blessed Virgin.

A Prayer to Our Guardian Angel

Angele Dei, qui custos es mei, me tibi commissum pietate superna, hodie illumina, custodi, rege, et guberna. Amen.

Angel of God, who art my guardian, enlighten, direct, and govern me this day, who have been committed to thee by the supernal clemency. Amen.

Grace before Meals

Benedicite, Dominus, nos et ea quae sumus sumpturi benedicat dextera Christi. In nomine Patris, etc.

Bless us, O Lord, as also the food of which we are about to partake. In the name of the Father, and of the Son, and of the Holy Ghost. Amen.

Grace after Meals

Agimus tibi gratias, omnipotens Deus, pro universis beneficiis tuis, qui vivis et regnas in saecula saeculorum. Amen. In nomine Patris, et Filii, etc.

We give thee thanks for all thy benefits, O Almighty God, who livest and reignest forever. Amen. In the name of the Father, and of the Son, etc.

A Prayer for the Dead

Fidelium animae, per misericordiam Dei, requiescant in pace. Amen.

May the souls of the faithful departed, through the mercy of God, rest in peace. Amen.

A Prayer Called the Angelus

℣. *Angelus Domini nuntiavit Mariae.*
℟. *Et concepit de Spiritu Sancto.*
Ave Maria, etc.
℣. *Ecce ancilla Domini.*
℟. *Fiat mihi secundum verbum tuum.*
Ave Maria, etc.
℣. *Et Verbum caro factum est.*
℟. *Et habitavit in nobis.*
Ave Maria, etc.
℣. *Ora pro nobis, sancta Dei Genitrix.*
℟. *Ut digni efficiamur promissionibus Christi.*
Oremus.

Gratiam tuam, quaesumus, Domine, mentibus nostris infunde; ut qui, angelo nuntiante, Christi Filii tui incarnationem cognovimus, per passionem ejus et crucem ad resurrectionis gloriam perducamur. Per eumdem Christum Dominum nostrum.
℟. *Amen.*

℣. The angel of the Lord declared unto Mary.
℟. And she conceived of the Holy Ghost.
Hail Mary, etc.
℣. Behold the handmaid of the Lord.
℟. Be it done unto me according to thy word.
Hail Mary, etc.
℣. And the Word was made flesh.
℟. And dwelt amongst us.

Hail Mary, etc.
℣. Pray for us, O holy Mother of God.
℟. That we may be made worthy of the promises of Christ.
Let us pray.

Pour forth, we beseech thee, O Lord, thy grace into our hearts; that we, to whom the incarnation of Christ thy Son, was made known by the message of an angel, may, by his passion and cross, be brought to the glory of his resurrection; through the same Christ our Lord. ℟. Amen.

Feasts of Obligation

ECCLESIASTICAL PROVINCES OF QUEBEC AND MONTREAL

(For the province of Ottawa, see further on)

Feasts of Obligation

All Sundays in the year.
The Circumcision of Our Lord, January 1st.
The Epiphany of Our Lord, January 6th.
The Annunciation of the Blessed Virgin Mary, March 25th.[4]
The Ascension of Our Lord.
Corpus Christi.
St. Peter and St. Paul, June 29th.
All Saints' day, November 1st.
The Immaculate Conception of the Blessed Virgin Mary, December 8th.
Christmas day, December 25th.

[4] When this festival is transferred to any other day than the 25th March, it ceases to be of obligation.

Solemnities Transferred to the Sunday

The feast of the Patron or Titular of parochial churches.
The Purification of the Blessed Virgin, February 2nd.
Saint Joseph, March 19th.
Saint John the Baptist, June 24th.
Saint Ann, July 26th.
The Assumption of the Blessed Virgin, August 15th.
The Nativity of the Blessed Virgin, September 8th.
Saint Michael, September 29th.

Fast Days of Obligation

The Ember days (Wednesday, Friday, and Saturday).
Every day in Lent, except Sundays.
Every Wednesday and Friday in Advent.
The Vigils of Christmas day, of Whitsunday, of St. Peter and St. Paul, and of the solemnity of the Assumption of the Blessed Virgin Mary, and of All Saints' day.

Days of Abstinence from Flesh Meat

1. The Ember days.
2. Every Friday in the year except it be Christmas day.
3. The vigils, on which a fast is commanded.
4. Ash Wednesday and the three following days.
5. Every Wednesday, Friday, and Saturday of the first five weeks of Lent.
6. Palm Sunday and the six days of Holy Week.
7. Every Wednesday and Friday in Advent.

Note.—a) On those days of Lent, on which flesh meat is allowed, it can be made use of at one meal only, but the use of fish and flesh is forbidden at the same meal.

b) Every day of abstinence during the year, it is allowed to prepare food with grease or lard, that is, to substitute these for butter or oil, in frying, cooking, or preparing fast meals.

c) On all fast days we may, in the morning, take about two ounces of bread with a little tea, coffee, chocolate, or other beverage.

ECCLESIASTICAL PROVINCE OF OTTAWA

Feasts of Obligation

All Sundays in the year.
The Circumcision of Our Lord, January 1st.
The Epiphany of Our Lord, January 6th.
The Ascension of Our Lord.
All Saints' day, November 1st.
The Immaculate Conception of the Blessed Virgin Mary, December 8th.
Christmas day, December 25th.

Solemnities Transferred to the Sunday

The feast of the Patron or Titular of parochial churches.
The Purification of the Blessed Virgin, February 2nd.
Saint Joseph, March 19th.
The Annunciation of the Blessed Virgin Mary, March 25th.
Corpus Christi.
Saint John the Baptist, June 24th.
St. Peter and St. Paul, June 29th.
Saint Ann, July 26th.
The Assumption of the Blessed Virgin, August 15th.
The Nativity of the Blessed Virgin, September 8th.
Saint Michael, Archangel, September 29th.

Fast Days of Obligation

The Ember days (Wednesday, Friday, and Saturday).
Every day in Lent, except Sundays.
Every Wednesday and Friday in Advent.
The Vigils of Christmas day, of Whitsunday, of All Saints' day, and the vigils of the feasts of Saint Peter and Saint Paul and of the Assumption of the Blessed Virgin Mary.

Days of Abstinence from Flesh Meat

The Ember days of the year.
Every Friday in the year except it be Christmas day.
The vigils on which it is commanded to fast.
Every Wednesday and Friday of Lent.
Holy Saturday.
Note.—The notes a, b, and c, which follow the days of fast and abstinence for the provinces of Quebec and Montreal, apply also to the Diocese of Ottawa.

The Quebec Catechism

On the End of Man

* 1. **Who created the world?**[5]
God is the Creator of heaven and earth and of all things visible and invisible.

* 2. **What is man?**
Man is a creature composed of body and soul, and made to the image and likeness of God.

3. **How is the soul like to God?**
The soul is like God because it is a spirit that will never die, and has understanding and free will.

4. **Why did God create you?**
God created me to know him, to love him, and to serve him in this world, and to be happy with him forever in the next.

5. **Should we take more care of our soul than of our body?**
Yes, we should take more care of our soul than of our body, because it is greatly superior to the body by nature, and because in losing it we lose God and everlasting happiness.

[5] The asterisk * indicates those questions which it will suffice to give to little children and to persons of very feeble memory.

* 6. **What must we do to save our souls?**

To save our souls, we must worship God by faith, hope, and charity; that is, we must believe in him, hope in him, and love him with all our heart.

* 7. **How shall we know the things which we are to believe and practice?**

We shall know the things which we are to believe and practice by receiving the teachings of the Catholic Church, through which God speaks to us.

* 8. **Where shall we find the chief truths which the Church teaches?**

We shall find the chief truths which the Church teaches in the Apostles' Creed.

* 9. **Say the Apostles' Creed.**

1. I believe in God, the Father Almighty, Creator of heaven and earth.
2. And in Jesus Christ, his only Son, our Lord.
3. Who was conceived by the Holy Ghost, born of the Virgin Mary.
4. Suffered under Pontius Pilate, was crucified, died, and was buried.
5. He descended into hell: the third day he arose again from the dead.
6. He ascended into heaven, sitteth at the right hand of God, the Father Almighty.
7. From thence he shall come to judge the living and the dead.
8. I believe in the Holy Ghost.
9. The holy Catholic Church, the communion of saints.
10. The forgiveness of sins.
11. The resurrection of the body.
12. And the life everlasting. Amen.

On God and His Perfections

* 10. **What is God?**

God is a Spirit infinitely perfect.

* 11. **Had God a beginning?**
God had no beginning; he always was and he always will be.

* 12. **Where is God?**
God is everywhere.

* 13. **If God is everywhere, why do we not see him?**
We do not see God, because he is a pure Spirit and cannot be seen with bodily eyes.

* 14. **Does God see us?**
Yes, God sees us and watches over us.

* 15. **Does God know all things?**
Yes, God knows all things, even our most secret thoughts, words, and actions.

* 16. **Can God do all things?**
Yes, God is all powerful, and nothing is impossible to him.

* 17. **Is God just, holy, and merciful?**
Yes, God is infinitely just, infinitely holy, infinitely merciful, because he is infinitely perfect.

On the Unity and Trinity of God

* 18. **Is there but one God?**
Yes, there is but one God.

* 19. **Why can there be but one God?**
There can be but one God, because God, being supreme and infinite, cannot have an equal.

* 20. **How many Persons are there in God?**
In God there are three divine Persons, really distinct, and equal in all things—the Father, the Son, and the Holy Ghost.

* 21. **Is the Father God?**
Yes; the Father is God and the first Person of the Blessed Trinity.

* 22. **Is the Son God?**
Yes; the Son is God and the second Person of the Blessed Trinity.

* 23. **Is the Holy Ghost God?**
Yes; the Holy Ghost is God and the third Person of the Blessed Trinity.

* 24. **What do you mean by "the Blessed Trinity"?**
By "the Blessed Trinity," I mean one God in three divine Persons.

25. **Are the three divine Persons equal in all things?**
Yes; the three divine Persons are equal in all things.

* 26. **Are the three divine Persons one and the same God?**
Yes; the three divine Persons are one and the same God; because they have one and the same divine nature.

27. **Can we understand how the three divine Persons are one and the same God?**
No; we cannot understand how the three divine Persons are one and the same God, because this is a mystery.

28. **What is a mystery?**
A mystery is a truth which we cannot understand, which we must believe, because God has revealed it.

On the Creation

* 29. **Who created heaven and earth?**
God created heaven and earth.

30. **How did God create heaven and earth?**
God created heaven and earth from nothing, by his Word only; that is, by a single act of his all-powerful will.

* 31. **Which are the chief creatures of God?**
The chief creatures of God are angels and men.

32. **Why did God create all the things which we see?**
God created all the things which we see to show his power, his wisdom, and his love.

* 33. **What use does God wish us to make of the things which he has created?**
God wishes that the use we make of all the things which he has created may contribute to his glory, the end for which they have been created.

34. **What are angels?**
Angels are pure spirits, created to the image and likeness of God, to adore and serve him.

* 35. **Do the angels concern themselves for us?**
Yes; angels have often been sent as messengers by God to man, and have also been appointed our guardians and protectors.

36. **Has God given a guardian angel to each of us?**
Yes; God has given a guardian angel to each of us, to protect us from evil and to help us to be good Christians.

37. **What are our duties toward our guardian angel?**
We should respect the presence of our guardian angel, show our gratitude for his loving care, invoke him with confidence in the hour of temptation, and avoid everything displeasing to God, which might remove him from us.

38. **Were the angels, when created by God, good and happy?**
Yes; the angels when created by God were good and happy.

39. **Did all the angels remain good and happy?**
No; all the angels did not remain good and happy; many of them sinned through pride and were driven into hell: they are called fallen angels or demons.

On Our First Parents and Their Fall

* 40. **Who were the first man and woman whom God created?**
The first man and woman whom God created were Adam and Eve, our first parents.

41. **Do we all descend from Adam and Eve?**
Yes; we all descend from Adam and Eve, and consequently we are all brothers.

* 42. **Were Adam and Eve innocent and holy when they came from the hand of God?**
Yes; Adam and Eve were innocent and holy when they came from the hand of God.

43. **What particular command did God give to Adam and Eve to test their obedience?**
To test the obedience of Adam and Eve, God forbade them to eat of a certain fruit which grew in the garden of paradise.

* 44. **How were Adam and Eve punished for their disobedience?**
Because of their disobedience, Adam and Eve lost their innocence and holiness, were cast out of the garden of paradise, and condemned to suffering and death.

* 45. **What befell us on account of the sin of our first parents?**
On account of the disobedience of our first parents, we all share in their sin and punishment.

46. **Did the sin of our first parents darken our understanding and weaken our will?**
Yes; the sin of our first parents darkened our understanding and weakened our will by giving us a propensity to evil.

* 47. **What is the sin called of which all men are born guilty?**
It is called "original sin," because we all come into the world with its stain on our soul.

48. **Do the effects of original sin on our understanding and will remain after original sin has been washed away by baptism?**
Yes; the darkness of our understanding and the weakness of our will remain, even after original sin has been washed away by baptism.

On Sin and Its Different Kinds

On Sin in General

* 49. **What is actual sin?**
Actual sin is that which is personally and willfully committed when the age of reason is attained.

50. **In how many ways is actual sin committed?**
Actual sin is committed by any voluntary thought, word, deed, or omission, opposed to the law of God.

* 51. **How many kinds of actual sin are there?**
There are two kinds of actual sin: mortal and venial.

* 52. **What is mortal sin?**
Mortal sin is that which kills the soul, by depriving it of sanctifying grace, by drawing down God's anger upon it, and by making it deserving of the pains of hell.

53. **When is a sin mortal?**
A sin is mortal when God is disobeyed in a grievous matter, with sufficient reflection, and full consent of the will.

* 54. **Are many mortal sins required to deserve hell?**
No; to deserve hell, one mortal sin is sufficient.

* 55. **What is venial sin?**
Venial sin is an act of disobedience toward God in matter of lesser importance, or in matter of greater importance, committed without sufficient reflection or full consent of the will.

* 56. **What are the effects of venial sin?**

Venial sin weakens spiritual life in us, lessens the love of God in our heart, and renders us worthy of temporal punishment in this life or in the next.

57. **Should we much dread venial sin?**

Yes; we should much dread venial sin, because it offends God, and often leads to mortal sin.

On the Capital Sins

* 58. **Which are the chief sources of sin?**

The chief sources of sin are seven: pride, covetousness, lust, envy, gluttony, anger, and sloth. They are commonly called capital sins.

59. **What is pride?**

Pride is an inordinate self-esteem which makes us prefer ourselves to others, and induces us to raise ourselves above them.

60. **What is covetousness?**

Covetousness is an inordinate attachment to earthly goods, and especially to money.

61. **What is lust?**

Lust is an intemperate love for carnal pleasures.

62. **What is envy?**

Envy is sorrow felt at our neighbor's prosperity, or guilty joy at his adversity.

63. **What is gluttony?**

Gluttony is unrestrained love for drinking and eating.

64. **Which is the most dangerous kind of gluttony?**

The most dangerous kind of gluttony is drunkenness, which destroys reason, makes man like a beast, and often causes his death.

65. **What means should be taken to avoid drunkenness?**
There are four excellent means of avoiding drunkenness: 1) to shun taverns; 2) to abstain from intoxicating liquor between meals; 3) to fly the company of those who are fond of drink; 4) to join a temperate society and follow its rules.

66. **What are the sins ordinarily occasioned by drunkenness?**
The sins ordinarily occasioned by drunkenness are: anger, oaths, blasphemies, obscene words, and impure actions.

67. **What is anger?**
Anger is a violent agitation of the soul, which moves us to revenge, or to repulse with violence what is displeasing to us.

68. **What is sloth?**
Sloth is an inordinate love of ease, which makes us neglect the duties of our station and religion, rather than do violence to our personal inclinations.

* 69. **What safeguards should be used against temptation?**
The safeguards to be used against temptation are: 1) prayer and the sacraments; 2) watchfulness and avoidance of occasions, especially of bad company.

On the Incarnation and Redemption

* 70. **Did God abandon man after he fell into sin?**
No; God did not abandon man after he fell into sin, but promised him a Redeemer, who was to satisfy for man's sin and open to him the gates of heaven.

* 71. **Who is this Redeemer promised by God to man?**
The Redeemer promised by God to man is our Lord and Savior Jesus Christ.

* 72. **Who is our Savior Jesus Christ?**
Our Savior Jesus Christ is the Son of God, the second Person of the Blessed Trinity, true God and true man.

73. **Why do you say that Jesus Christ is true God?**
I say that Jesus Christ is true God, because he is the only Son of God, equal to his Father in all things, and consequently possessing the same divine nature.

74. **Why do you say that Jesus Christ is true man?**
I say that Jesus Christ is true man, because he was born of the Blessed Virgin Mary, and has a body and soul like ours.

75. **Why do you say that Jesus Christ is our Savior?**
I say that Jesus Christ is our Savior because he redeemed us, and because his Father gave us to him.

76. **Are there two natures in Jesus Christ?**
Yes; there are two natures in Jesus Christ: the divine nature and the human.

77. **Is there more than one Person in Jesus Christ?**
No; in Jesus Christ there is only one Person, the divine Person of the Son of God.

78. **Was Jesus Christ always God?**
Yes, Jesus Christ was always God as he is the second Person of the Blessed Trinity, equal to his Father from all eternity.

79. **Was Jesus Christ always man?**
No; Jesus Christ was not always man, but became man at the time of his incarnation.

* 80. **What do you mean by "the incarnation"?**
The incarnation is the union of the human nature with the divine nature in the Person of the Son of God.

* 81. **How was the mystery of the incarnation effected?**
The mystery of the incarnation was effected in the womb of the Blessed Virgin Mary by the operation of the Holy Ghost; that is to say, by a miracle of divine omnipotence.

82. **Why did the Son of God become man?**
The Son of God became man to redeem us from the slavery of sin, to deliver us from the pains of hell, and to merit eternal life for us.

83. **Did the Son of God become man immediately after the sin of our first parents?**
No; he was then only promised to them as a Redeemer.

84. **How could they be saved who lived before the incarnation of the Son of God?**
They who lived before the incarnation of the Son of God could be saved by believing in a Redeemer to come, by observing the natural law written in their hearts, and by the grace granted to them through the merits of the Redeemer to come.

* 85. **On what day did the Son of God become man?**
The Son of God became man in the womb of the Blessed Virgin Mary, at Nazareth, on the day of the annunciation, when the angel Gabriel announced to the Blessed Virgin that she would be the Mother of God.

* 86. **On what day was Jesus Christ born?**
Jesus Christ was born on Christmas day, in a stable at Bethlehem.

87. **Why did Jesus Christ remain thirty-three years on earth?**
Jesus Christ remained thirty-three years on earth to show us the way to heaven by his examples and teaching, and to merit graces for us.

88. **What is the meaning of the word *gospel*?**
The word *gospel* means "good tidings."

On Our Lord's Passion, Death, Resurrection, and Ascension

* 89. **What did Jesus Christ suffer for us?**
After his agony in the Garden of Olives, Jesus Christ was betrayed by Judas, abandoned by his apostles, covered with opprobrium, scourged, crowned with thorns, and died nailed to the cross.

* 90. **On what day did Jesus Christ die?**
Jesus Christ died on Good Friday, about the third hour after noon.

91. **Why do you call that day "good" on which Jesus Christ died so cruel a death?**
We call it "good," because on that day Jesus Christ, by his death, showed his great love for man, and purchased for him every grace.

92. **Where and how did Jesus Christ die?**
Jesus Christ died on Calvary, nailed to the cross, and between two thieves.

93. **Why did Jesus Christ die?**
Jesus Christ died to redeem all men.

* 94. **How did Jesus Christ redeem us?**
Jesus Christ redeemed us by dying for us, as man, and by giving, as God, infinite value to his sufferings and death.

95. **What lessons do we learn from the sufferings and death of Jesus Christ?**
From the sufferings and death of Jesus Christ, we learn the great evil of sin, the hatred God bears to it, and the necessity of satisfying for it.

96. **What do you call the mystery of the death of Jesus Christ on the cross for us?**
The mystery of the death of Jesus Christ on the cross for our sake is called "the mystery of the redemption."

97. **Whither did Jesus Christ's soul go after his death?**
Jesus Christ's soul, separated from his body, descended into hell, that is to say, into limbo, where the souls of the just, since the creation of the world, were detained.

98. **Why did Jesus Christ descend into limbo?**
Jesus Christ descended into limbo to display his power, and to impart the fruits of his passion to the souls of the just imprisoned there.

99. **Where was Jesus Christ's body while his soul was in limbo?**
While Jesus Christ's soul was in limbo, his body was in the holy sepulchre.

* 100. **On what day did Jesus Christ rise from the dead?**
Jesus Christ rose from the dead, glorious and immortal, on Easter Sunday, the third day after his death.

101. **How did Jesus Christ rise from the dead?**
Jesus Christ rose from the dead through his own omnipotence, as he had announced it.

* 102. **How long did Jesus Christ stay on earth after his resurrection?**
After his resurrection, Jesus Christ frequently appeared to his apostles, during forty days, to show them that he was really risen from the dead, and to finish instructing them.

* 103. **After Jesus Christ had remained forty days on earth, whither did he go?**
The fortieth day after his resurrection, Jesus Christ ascended, by his own power, into heaven, in presence of a great number of his disciples; that day is called Ascension day.

104. **Where is Jesus Christ in heaven?**
In heaven, Jesus Christ sits at the right hand of God the Father Almighty.

105. **What do you mean by these words: "Sits at the right hand of God the Father Almighty"?**
By these words, I mean that Jesus Christ, as God, is equal to his Father in all things, and that, as man, he is in the highest place in heaven next to God.

On the Holy Ghost and His Descent upon the Apostles

* 106. **Who is the Holy Ghost?**
The Holy Ghost is the third Person of the Blessed Trinity.

107. **From whom does the Holy Ghost proceed?**
The Holy Ghost proceeds from the Father and the Son.

108. **Is the Holy Ghost equal to the Father and the Son?**
Yes, the Holy Ghost is equal to the Father and the Son, and he is the same God as the Father and the Son, since He possesses the same infinite perfections.

* 109. **On what day did the Holy Ghost come down upon the apostles?**
The Holy Ghost came down upon the apostles on Pentecost Sunday, ten days after the ascension of Jesus Christ.

110. **How did the Holy Ghost come down upon the apostles?**
The Holy Ghost came down upon the apostles in the form of tongues of fire.

111. **Who sent the Holy Ghost upon the apostles?**
The Holy Ghost was sent upon the apostles by God the Father and God the Son.

* 112. **Why was the Holy Ghost sent upon the apostles?**
The Holy Ghost was sent upon the apostles to enlighten them, to strengthen them, and to enable them to preach the gospel, and sanctify the Church.

113. **Will the Holy Ghost abide with the Church forever?**
The Holy Ghost will abide with the Church forever, to guide it in the way of holiness and truth.

114. **Does not the Holy Ghost also communicate with us?**
Yes, the Holy Ghost communicates with each one of us, by those graces of which we stand in need, and especially in the sacrament of confirmation.

On the Effects of the Redemption

* 115. **Which are the chief effects of the redemption?**

The chief effects of the redemption are: 1) the satisfaction of God's justice for our sins, by the sufferings and death of Jesus Christ; 2) the gaining of grace for men.

* 116. **What is grace?**

Grace is a supernatural gift of God bestowed on us, through his mere bounty and the merits of Jesus Christ, for our salvation.

117. **How many kinds of grace are there?**

There are two kinds of grace: sanctifying or habitual grace, and actual grace.

* 118. **What is sanctifying grace?**

Sanctifying grace is that which dwells in the soul, and makes it holy and pleasing to God.

* 119. **Can we lose sanctifying grace?**

Yes, one mortal sin suffices to make us lose sanctifying grace.

120. **Which are the theological virtues?**

The theological virtues are faith, hope, and charity, the immediate object of which is God.

* 121. **What is faith?**

Faith is a divine virtue by which we firmly believe the truths which God has revealed, and which he teaches us by his Church.

* 122. **What is hope?**

Hope is a divine virtue by which we firmly trust that God, through his bounty, will give us eternal life and the graces necessary to obtain it.

* 123. **What is charity?**

Charity is a divine virtue by which we love God above all things, and our neighbor as ourselves for the love of God.

124. **What do you mean by "our neighbor"?**

By this designation, I mean all men, even our enemies.

* 125. **What is actual grace?**

Actual grace is that passing help by which God enlightens our mind and moves our will to avoid evil and do good.

* 126. **Is grace necessary to salvation?**

Yes, grace is absolutely necessary, and without it we can do nothing to merit heaven.

127. **Can we resist the grace of God?**

We can, and unfortunately often do resist the grace of God.

128. **What is the grace of perseverance?**

The grace of perseverance is a particular gift of God, which maintains us or enables us to continue in the state of grace till death.

On the Church

* 129. **Which are the means given to men to enable them to share in the fruits of the redemption?**
The means given to men to enable them to share in the fruits of the redemption are the Church and the sacraments.

* 130. **What is the Church?**
The Church is the congregation of all those who profess the faith of Christ, partake of the same sacraments, and are governed by their lawful pastors under one visible head.

* 131. **Who is the invisible head of the Church?**
Jesus Christ is the invisible head of the Church.

*132. **Who is the visible head of the Church?**
Our holy father the pope, the bishop of Rome, who is the vicar of Christ on earth, and the visible head of the Church.

133. **Why is the pope, the bishop of Rome, the visible head of the Church?**
The pope, the bishop of Rome, is the visible head of the Church, because he is the successor of St. Peter, whom Christ made the chief of the apostles and the visible head of the Church.

134. **Who are the successors of the other apostles?**
The successors of the other apostles are the bishops of the holy Catholic Church.

135. **Did Jesus Christ establish several Churches?**
Jesus Christ established only one Church, the government of which he gave to Saint Peter and his successors.

136. **Why did Jesus Christ found his Church?**
Jesus Christ founded his Church to teach, govern, sanctify, and save all men.

137. **Are all men bound to belong to this one Church established by Jesus Christ?**
Yes, all men are bound to belong to this one Church founded by Jesus Christ, and he who knows the Catholic Church to be the true Church and remains out of it cannot be saved.

On the Attributes and Marks of the Church

138. **Which are the attributes of the Church?**
The attributes of the Church are three: authority, infallibility, and indefectibility.

139. **What do you mean by "the authority of the Church"?**
By "the authority of the Church," I mean the mission, right, and power which the pope and the bishops, as the successors of the apostles, have received from Jesus Christ to preach the gospel and to govern the faithful.

140. **What do you mean by "the infallibility of the Church"?**
By "the infallibility of the Church," I mean that prerogative which Jesus Christ gave to his Church, which renders it free from error when it teaches a doctrine of faith or morals.

141. **When is the teaching of the Church infallible?**
The teaching of the Church is infallible when the pope alone, or the pope and bishops, speaking to all the faithful, define and proclaim a doctrine of faith or morals.

142. **What do you mean by "the indefectibility of the Church"?**
By "the indefectibility of the Church," I mean that the Church, as Jesus Christ founded it, will last till the end of time.

143. **In whom are these attributes found in their fullness?**
These attributes are found in their fullness in the pope, whose authority and infallibility will last to the end of time.

* 144. **What are the marks or notes by which the Church may be known?**
The Church has four marks or notes by which it may be known: it is one; it is holy; it is catholic; it is apostolic.

145. **How is the Church one?**
The Church is one because all its members profess the same faith, are all in one communion, and are all under one head.

146. **Why do you call the Church "holy"?**
I call the Church "holy" because its founder, Jesus Christ, is holy, and because it can sanctify us by its teaching and its sacraments.

147. **How is the Church catholic or universal?**
The Church is catholic or universal because it will not cease to exist till the end of time, and because it teaches all nations, and maintains all truths necessary to salvation.

148. **How is the Church apostolic?**
The Church is apostolic because it was founded by Jesus Christ on his apostles, and is governed by their lawful successors, and because it has taught and always will teach their doctrine.

* 149. **Are these marks and attributes to be found elsewhere besides in the Roman Catholic Church?**
These marks and attributes can only be found in the holy Roman Catholic Church.

On the Sacraments in General

* 150. **What is a sacrament?**
A sacrament is a sensible sign instituted by Jesus Christ to give grace.

* 151. **How many sacraments are there?**
There are seven sacraments: baptism, confirmation, Eucharist, penance, extreme unction, holy orders, and matrimony.

* 152. **Whence have the sacraments the power of giving grace?**
The sacraments have the power of giving grace from the merits of Jesus Christ.

153. **What grace do the sacraments give?**
Some of the sacraments give to sinners sanctifying grace which justifies them, and brings them from the death of sin to the life of grace; others increase sanctifying grace in souls possessing supernatural life.

154. **Which are the sacraments that give to sinners the grace of justification?**
The sacraments that give to sinners the grace of justification are baptism and penance.

155. **Why are baptism and penance called "sacraments of the dead"?**
Baptism and penance are called "sacraments of the dead" because they wipe out sin which is the death of the soul, and give grace which is its life.

156. **Which are the sacraments that increase sanctifying grace in our soul?**
The sacraments that increase sanctifying grace in our soul are five: confirmation, Holy Eucharist, extreme unction, holy orders, and matrimony; they are called "sacraments of the living."

157. **Why are these five sacraments called "sacraments of the living"?**
These five sacraments are called "sacraments of the living" because they who receive them worthily are already living the life of grace.

158. **What sin does he commit who receives the sacraments of the living in mortal sin?**
He who willingly receives a sacrament of the living in mortal sin commits a sacrilege, which is a very great sin, because it is an abuse of a sacred thing.

* 159. **Besides sanctifying grace, do the sacraments give any other grace?**
Yes; besides sanctifying grace, the sacraments give another grace called "sacramental."

160. **What is sacramental grace?**
Sacramental grace is a special help which God gives to attain the end for which he instituted each sacrament.

161. **Do the sacraments always give grace?**
Yes, the sacraments always give grace; for this reason, we should always receive them with good dispositions.

* 162. **Which are the sacraments that can be received only once?**
The sacraments which can be received only once are baptism, confirmation, and holy orders.

* 163. **Why can we not receive baptism, confirmation, and holy orders more than once?**
We cannot receive baptism, confirmation, and holy orders more than once, because they imprint in the soul a character or spiritual mark, which remains forever.

164. **Why does this character remain in the soul even after death?**
This character remains in the soul even after death, for the honor and glory of those who are saved, for the shame and punishment of those who are damned.

On Baptism

* 165. **What is baptism?**
Baptism is a sacrament which cleanses us from original sin, makes us Christians, children of God, and heirs to heaven.

* 166. **Are actual sins also remitted by baptism?**
Actual sins and all the punishment due to them are remitted by baptism, if sincere sorrow be felt for having committed them.

* 167. **Is baptism necessary to salvation?**
Yes, baptism is necessary to salvation.

* 168. **Who can administer baptism?**
The priest is the ordinary minister of baptism; but, in case of necessity, anyone who has the use of reason may baptize.

* 169. **How is baptism given?**
Whoever baptizes should pour water on the head of the person to be baptized, and say, while pouring the water: "I baptize thee in the name of the Father, and of the Son, and of the Holy Ghost."

170. **How many kinds of baptism are there?**
There are three kinds of baptism: baptism of water, of desire, and of blood.

171. **What is baptism of water?**
Baptism of water is that which is given by pouring ordinary water on the head of the person to be baptized, and saying at the same time: "I baptize thee in the name of the Father, and of the Son, and of the Holy Ghost."

172. **When baptism of water cannot be received, can it be replaced by baptism of desire?**
Yes; when baptism of water cannot be received, it may be replaced by the desire of receiving it when possible, with sincere sorrow for past sins, and the resolution of observing the law of God.

173. **What is baptism of blood?**
Baptism of blood is martyrdom suffered for the faith of Jesus Christ, or for some Christian virtue, with sincere sorrow for sins committed.

174. **Do baptism of desire and baptism of blood produce the same effects as baptism of water?**
Baptism of desire or baptism of blood renders us worthy of entering heaven, but does not imprint a character on the soul.

175. **What do we renounce before receiving baptism?**
Before receiving baptism, we forever renounce the devil, his works and pomps, that is to say, sin of every kind and false maxims.

176. **Why is the name of a saint given to him who receives baptism?**
The name of a saint is given in baptism in order that the person baptized may imitate his virtues and have him for a protector.

177. **Why are godfathers and godmothers given in baptism?**
Godfathers and godmothers are given in baptism in order that they may promise, in the name of the child, what the child itself would promise if it had the use of reason.

178. **What are the obligations of a godfather and a godmother?**
The obligations of a godfather and a godmother are: 1) to instruct the child in its religious duties, if the parents neglect to do so or die; 2) to see, if necessary, that the promises made at baptism are accomplished.

On Confirmation

* 179. **What is confirmation?**
Confirmation is a sacrament through which we receive the Holy Ghost, who gives us strength to confess our faith without fear, and to lead a holy life, in spite of the obstacles put in our way by the devil.

* 180. **By whom is confirmation administered?**
Confirmation is administered by the bishop, or by a priest to whom the pope has granted special powers.

* 181. **How is confirmation administered?**
The bishop extends his hands over those who are to be confirmed, prays that they may receive the Holy Ghost, anoints the forehead of each with holy chrism, and gives each a slight blow on the cheek, saying: "Peace be with you."

182. **What is holy chrism?**
Holy chrism is a mixture of olive oil and balm consecrated by the bishop, every year, on Holy Thursday.

* 183. **What does the bishop say in anointing the person he confirms?**
In anointing the person he confirms, the bishop says, "I sign thee with the sign of the cross, and I confirm thee with the chrism of salvation, in the name of the Father, and of the Son, and of the Holy Ghost."

184. **What is meant by anointing the forehead with chrism in the form of a cross?**
By anointing the forehead with chrism in the form of a cross is meant that the Christian who is confirmed must openly profess and practice his faith, never be ashamed of it, and rather die than deny it.

185. **Why does the bishop give the person he confirms a slight blow on the cheek?**
The bishop gives the person he confirms a slight blow on the cheek to put him in mind that he must be ready to suffer everything, even death, for the sake of Christ.

* 186. **To receive confirmation worthily, is it necessary to be in the state of grace?**
Yes; to receive confirmation worthily, it is necessary to be in the state of grace.

187. **What special preparation should be made to receive confirmation?**
To receive confirmation, persons should know, as well as possible, the chief mysteries of faith, the duties of a Christian, and especially what relates to the nature and effects of the sacrament of confirmation.

* 188. **Is it a sin to neglect confirmation?**
Yes; it is a sin to neglect confirmation, especially in these evil days, when faith and morals are exposed to such great dangers.

On the Effects of Confirmation

189. **What are the effects of confirmation?**
The effects of confirmation are an increase of sanctifying grace, the strengthening of our faith, and the gifts of the Holy Ghost.

190. **Which are the gifts of the Holy Ghost?**
The seven gifts of the Holy Ghost are wisdom, understanding, counsel, fortitude, knowledge, piety, and the fear of the Lord.

191. **Why is the gift of wisdom given us?**
The gift of wisdom is given us that we may have greater relish for the things of God, and that we may direct all our actions to his honor and glory.

192. **What is the gift of understanding?**
The gift of understanding is that which makes more clearly known to us the truths which we must believe and practice.

193. **Why do we receive the gift of counsel?**
We receive the gift of counsel to warn us of the deceits of the devil, and of the dangers to salvation.

194. **Why do we receive the gift of fortitude?**
We receive the gift of fortitude to strengthen us to do the will of God in all things.

195. **What is the gift of knowledge?**
The gift of knowledge is that which enables us to discover the will of God in all things.

196. **What do you mean by the "gift of piety"?**
By the "gift of piety," I mean that which makes us love God as a Father, and obey him because we love him.

197. **Why is the gift of fear of the Lord given us?**
We receive the gift of fear of the Lord to fill us with a great horror of sin.

On the Sacrament of Penance

198. **What is the sacrament of penance?**
Penance is a sacrament which remits the sins committed after baptism.

199. **Does the sacrament of penance restore to the soul the friendship of God when it cleanses it from its sins?**
Yes; the sacrament of penance restores to the soul the friendship of God when it cleanses it from its sins.

* 200. **When do we receive the sacrament of penance?**
We receive the sacrament of penance when the priest gives absolution.

201. **Have priests the power of remitting sins committed after baptism?**
Yes; priests have the power of remitting sins committed after baptism, because Jesus Christ gave it to them, when he said to his apostles: "Receive ye the Holy Ghost. Whose sins you shall forgive, they are forgiven them; whose sins you shall retain, they are retained."[6]

202. **How do priests exercise the power of forgiving sins?**
Priests exercise the power of forgiving sins by hearing the confession of sins, and granting pardon for them, as ministers of God and in his name.

* 203. **What must we do to receive the sacrament of penance worthily?**
To receive the sacrament of penance worthily, we must do five things: 1) we must examine our conscience; 2) we must have sorrow for our sins; 3) we must make a firm resolution never more to offend God; 4) we must confess our sins to the priest; 5) we must accept the penance which the priest gives us.

[6] Jn 20:22-23

204. **What is the examination of conscience?**

The examination of conscience is an earnest effort to recall to mind all the sins we have committed since our last worthy confession.

* 205. **What should we do to make a good examination of conscience?**

To make a good examination of conscience, we should call to mind in succession the commandments of God, the precepts of the Church, the seven capital sins, and the particular duties of our state in life, to find out the sins we have committed.

206. **What should we do before beginning the examination of conscience?**

Before beginning the examination of conscience, we should pray to God to give us light to know our sins, and grace to detest them.

On Contrition

* 207. **What is contrition?**

Contrition is sorrow for and hatred of sins committed, with a firm purpose of sinning no more.

* 208. **Make an act of contrition?**

An act of contrition.—"O my God, I am heartly sorry for having offended thee, because thou art infinitely good and infinitely amiable, and because sin displeases thee; pardon me through the merits of Jesus Christ, my Savior; I purpose, by the help of thy holy grace, never more to offend thee and to do penance."

* 209. **Is contrition absolutely necessary to obtain pardon for our sins?**

Yes; contrition is absolutely necessary to obtain pardon for our sins.

210. **What kind of sorrow should we have for our sins?**
The sorrow we should have for our sins should be interior, supernatural, universal, and sovereign.

211. **What do you mean by saying that our sorrow should be interior?**
When I say that our sorrow should be interior, I mean that it should come from the heart, and not merely from the lips.

212. **What do you mean by saying that our sorrow should be supernatural?**
When I say that our sorrow should be supernatural, I mean that it should be prompted by the grace of God, and excited by motives which spring from faith, and not by merely natural motives.

213. **What do you mean by saying that our sorrow should be universal?**
When I say that our sorrow should be universal, I mean that we should be sorry for all our sins, at least for all our mortal sins without exception.

214. **What do you mean when you say that our sorrow should be sovereign?**
When I say that our sorrow should be sovereign, I mean that we should grieve more for having offended God than for any other evil that can befall us.

215. **Why should we be sorry for our sins?**
We should be sorry for our sins for three reasons: 1) because sin is the greatest of evils and an offense against God our Creator, Father, and Redeemer; 2) because it caused the death of Jesus Christ; 3) because it deprives us of the happiness of heaven and renders us deserving of the eternal torments of hell.

216. **How many kinds of contrition are there?**
There are two kinds of contrition: perfect contrition and imperfect contrition.

* 217. **What is perfect contrition?**

Perfect contrition is that which fills us with sorrow and hatred for sin, because it offends God, who is infinitely good in himself and worthy of all love.

* 218. **What is imperfect contrition?**

Imperfect contrition is that by which we regret and hate sin, because, by it, we lose heaven and deserve hell; or because sin is so hateful in itself that we are ashamed at having committed it.

219. **Is imperfect contrition sufficient for a worthy confession?**

Yes; imperfect contrition is sufficient for a worthy confession, but we should endeavor to have perfect contrition.

* 220. **What should we do if, in danger of death, we feel guilty of mortal sin, and cannot obtain a priest to hear our confession?**

If, in danger of death, we feel guilty of mortal sin and cannot obtain a priest to hear our confession, we must excite ourselves to an act of perfect contrition, with the firm purpose of confessing our sins as soon as possible.

221. **What do you mean by "a firm purpose of sinning no more"?**

By "a firm purpose of sinning no more," I mean a fixed resolve not only to avoid all mortal sin, but also its near occasions.

* 222. **What do you mean by "the near occasions of sin"?**

By "the near occasions of sin," I mean all the persons, places, and things that may easily lead us into sin.

On Confession and Satisfaction

* 223. **What is confession?**
Confession is the telling of our sins to a duly authorized priest, in order to obtain forgiveness.

* 224. **What sins are we bound to confess?**
We are bound to confess all our mortal sins, but it is well also to confess our venial sins.

225. **Which are the chief qualities of a good confession?**
The chief qualities of a good confession are three: it must be humble, sincere, and entire.

226. **When is our confession humble?**
Our confession is humble when we accuse ourselves of our sins, with a deep sense of shame and sorrow for having offended God.

227. **When is our confession sincere?**
Our confession is sincere when we tell our sins honestly and truthfully, neither exaggerating nor excusing them.

228. **When is our confession entire?**
Our confession is entire when we tell the number and kinds of our sins and the circumstances which change their nature.

* 229. **What should we do if we cannot remember the number of our sins?**
If we cannot remember the number of our sins, we should tell the number as nearly as possible, and say how often we have sinned in a day, a week, or a month, and how long the evil habit has lasted.

* 230. **Is our confession worthy if, without our fault, we forget to confess a mortal sin?**
If without our fault we forget to confess a mortal sin, our confession is worthy, and the sin is forgiven; but if, in a future confession, it come to our mind, it must be told.

231. **Is it a grievous offense willfully to conceal a mortal sin in confession?**
Yes, it is a grievous offense willfully to conceal a mortal sin in confession, because we thereby tell a lie to the Holy Ghost, and make our confession null and sacrilegious.

* 232. **What must he do who has willfully concealed a mortal sin in confession?**
He who has willfully concealed a mortal sin in confession must not only confess it, but also his sacrilege, and he must repeat all the sins he has committed since his last worthy confession.

* 233. **Why does the priest give us a penance after confession?**
The priest gives us a penance after confession that we may satisfy God for the temporal punishment due to our sins, and to deter the penitent from again committing them.

234. **Does the sacrament of penance remit all punishment due to sin?**
The sacrament of penance remits the eternal punishment due to sin, but it does not always remit the temporal punishment which God requires as satisfaction for our sins.

235. **Why does God require a temporal punishment as a satisfaction for sin?**
God requires a temporal punishment as a satisfaction for sin to teach us the great evil of sin, and to deter us from committing it again.

236. **Which are the chief means by which we satisfy God for the temporal punishment due to sin?**
The chief means by which we satisfy God for the temporal punishment due to sin are: prayer, fasting, almsgiving, all spiritual and corporal works

of mercy, the patient suffering of the ills of life, and the penance imposed by the confessor.

237. **Which are the chief spiritual works of mercy?**
The chief spiritual works of mercy are: to exhort the sinner to repentance, to instruct the ignorant, to give good counsel, to comfort the sorrowful, to bear wrongs patiently, to forgive all injuries, and to pray for the living and the dead.

238. **Which are the chief corporal works of mercy?**
The chief corporal works of mercy are seven: to feed the hungry, to give drink to the thirsty, to clothe the naked, to ransom the captive, to harbor the traveler, to visit the sick, and to bury the dead.

On the Manner of Making a Good Confession

* 239. **What should we do on entering the confessional?**
On entering the confessional, we should kneel, make the sign of the cross, and recite the *confiteor* ("I confess to Almighty God...") to the end, or only: "I confess to Almighty God and to you, Father, that I have sinned."

* 240. **After the *confiteor*, what must we do?**
After the *confiteor*, we must 1) tell the priest the time of our last confession, whether we received absolution and performed the penance enjoined; we must 2) confess all the mortal sins we have committed since the last time we received absolution, and the venial sins we may wish to mention, saying before the mention of each sin: "I accuse myself, Father, of..."

* 241. **What must we do after confessing our sins?**

After confessing our sins, we say: "I accuse myself moreover of many other sins which at present I cannot recall to memory, and of all the sins of my past life; for them I ask forgiveness of God, and of you, Father, penance and absolution." We then listen attentively to the advice which the confessor may think proper to give.

* 242. **What must we do when the confessor questions us?**

When the confessor questions us we must answer truthfully and clearly.

* 243. **Are we allowed to accuse one or several faults of which we have accused ourselves in other confessions?**

Yes; and it is sometimes well to renew the accusation of certain sins, in order better to excite ourselves to contrition, and to assure the validity of the sacrament.

* 244. **What should we do while the priest is giving us absolution?**

While the priest is giving us absolution, we should, from our heart, renew the act of contrition.

* 245. **What should we do after having received absolution?**

After having received absolution, we should humbly retire, thank God for having forgiven us, and perform our penance as soon as possible.

On Indulgences

* 246. **What is an indulgence?**

An indulgence is the remission, in whole or in part, of the temporal punishment due to the sin which has been forgiven.

247. **Is an indulgence a forgiveness of sin, or a license to commit sin?**
An indulgence is not a forgiveness of sin, nor a license to commit sin, as protestants pretend; indeed, he who is in a state of mortal sin cannot gain an indulgence.

248. **How many kinds of indulgences are there?**
There are two kinds of indulgences: the plenary indulgence and the partial indulgence.

* 249. **What is a plenary indulgence?**
A plenary indulgence is the full remission of the temporal punishment due to sin.

250. **What is a partial indulgence?**
A partial indulgence is the remission of a part of the temporal punishment due to sin.

251. **How does the Church, by means of indulgences, remit the temporal punishment due to sin?**
The Church, by means of indulgences, remits the temporal punishment due to sin, by applying to us the merits of Jesus Christ, and the superabundant satisfactions of the Blessed Virgin Mary and of the saints; which satisfactions form its spiritual treasury.

* 252. **What must we do to gain an indulgence?**
To gain an indulgence, we must be in the state of grace, and perform the works enjoined by him who grants the indulgence.

On the Holy Eucharist

* 253. **What is the Holy Eucharist?**
The Holy Eucharist is a sacrament which really and in truth contains the body, blood, soul, and divinity of our Lord Jesus Christ, under the appearances of bread and wine.

254. **When did Jesus Christ institute the Holy Eucharist?**
Jesus Christ instituted the Holy Eucharist at the last supper, on Holy Thursday, the eve of his death.

255. **Who were present when Jesus Christ instituted the Holy Eucharist?**
The twelve apostles were present when Jesus Christ instituted the Holy Eucharist.

256. **How did our Lord institute the Holy Eucharist?**
Our Lord instituted the Holy Eucharist by taking bread, blessing, breaking, and giving to his apostles, saying: "Take ye and eat. This is my body";[7] and then by taking the cup of wine, blessing and giving it, saying to them: "Drink ye all of this. This is my blood which shall be shed for the remission of sins. Do this for a commemoration of me."[8]

257. **What happened when our Lord said: "This is my body; this is my blood"?**
When our Lord said, "This is my body," the substance of the bread was changed into the substance of his body; when he said, "This is my blood," the substance of the wine was changed into the substance of his blood.

[7] Mt 26:26; 1 Cor 11:24
[8] Cf. Mt 26:27-28; 1 Cor 11:25

258. **Is Jesus Christ whole and entire under the form of bread and under the form of wine?**
Yes, Jesus Christ is whole and entire under the form of bread and under the form of wine; nay, he is whole and entire under either species.

259. **What remained of the bread and wine after their substance had been changed into the substance of the body and blood of Jesus Christ?**
After the substance of the bread and wine had been changed into the substance of the body and blood of Jesus Christ, there remained only the appearances of bread and wine.

* 260. **What do you mean by "the appearances of bread and wine"?**
By "the appearances of bread and wine," I mean whatsoever touches the senses, such as the figure, the color, the taste.

261. **What is this change of the bread and wine into the body and blood of Jesus Christ called?**
This change of the bread and wine into the body and blood of Jesus Christ is called "transubstantiation."

262. **How was the substance of the bread and wine changed into the substance of the body and blood of Jesus Christ?**
The substance of the bread and wine was changed into the substance of the body and blood of Jesus Christ by his almighty power.

263. **Does this change of bread and wine into the body and blood of Jesus Christ continue to be made in the Church?**
Yes, this change of bread and wine into the body and blood of Jesus Christ continues to be made in the Church by Jesus Christ through the ministry of his priests.

* 264. **When did Jesus Christ give to his priests the power of changing bread and wine into his body and blood?**
Jesus Christ gave to his priests the power of changing bread and wine into his body and blood when he said to the apostles: "Do this in commemoration of me."[9]

* 265. **When do the priests exercise this power of changing bread and wine into the body and blood of Jesus Christ?**
The priests exercise this power of changing bread and wine into the body and blood of Jesus Christ when, in the Mass, they pronounce the words of consecration, which are Christ's own words: "This is my body; this is my blood."

266. **Should we adore the body and blood of our Lord in the Holy Eucharist?**
Yes, we should adore the body and blood of our Lord in the Holy Eucharist, because his body and blood are inseparably united to his divinity.

267. **Does Jesus Christ leave heaven in order to be present in the Holy Eucharist?**
No, Jesus Christ does not leave heaven in order to be present in the Holy Eucharist: he is both in heaven and in the Holy Eucharist.

On the Ends for Which the Holy Eucharist Was Instituted

* 268. **Why did Jesus Christ institute the Holy Eucharist?**
Jesus Christ instituted the Holy Eucharist: 1) to unite us to himself and to testify his love for us; 2) to increase sanctifying grace in our soul, and to

[9] Lk 22:19; Cf. 1 Cor 11:24-25

strengthen us against evil; 3) to be a pledge of everlasting life and to fit our bodies for a glorious resurrection.

269. **How are we united to Jesus Christ in the Holy Eucharist?**
We are united to Jesus Christ in the Holy Eucharist by means of Holy Communion.

* 270. **What is Holy Communion?**
Holy Communion is the receiving of the body and blood of Jesus Christ.

* 271. **What is necessary to make a good Communion?**
To make a good Communion, it is necessary to be in the state of sanctifying grace, and to be fasting from midnight.

* 272. **Does he who receives Communion in mortal sin receive the body and blood of Christ?**
He who receives Communion in mortal sin receives the body and blood of Christ, but does not receive his grace, and he is guilty of a great sacrilege.

273. **Is it enough to be free from mortal sin to receive plentifully the graces of Holy Communion?**
No, to receive plentifully the graces of Holy Communion, it is not enough to be free from mortal sin, but we should be free from all affection for venial sin, and should make acts of lively faith, of firm hope, and ardent love.

* 274. **What is the necessary fast for Holy Communion?**
The necessary fast for Holy Communion is the abstaining from midnight from everything which is taken as food or drink.

275. **Is anyone ever allowed to receive Holy Communion when not fasting?**
Anyone in danger of death is allowed to receive Holy Communion when not fasting.

276. **When are we bound to receive Holy Communion?**
We are bound to receive Holy Communion, under pain of mortal sin, during the Easter time and when in danger of death.

277. **Is it well to receive Holy Communion frequently?**
Yes, it is well and even often necessary to receive Holy Communion frequently, because it increases grace in our souls, and strengthens us against evil.

* 278. **What should we do after Communion?**
After Communion, we should spend some time in adoring and thanking our Lord, and in asking him for the graces we need.

On the Sacrifice of the Mass

* 279. **What is the Mass?**
The Mass is the unbloody sacrifice of the body and blood of Jesus Christ, consecrated on the altar, and offered to God by the priest.

280. **What is a sacrifice?**
A sacrifice is the offering of an object by a priest to God alone, and the consuming of it to acknowledge that he is the Creator and Lord of all things.

* 281. **Is the Mass the same sacrifice as that of the cross?**
Yes, the Mass is the same sacrifice as that of the cross.

282. **How is the Mass the same sacrifice as that of the cross?**
The Mass is the same sacrifice as that of the cross, because the offering and the priest are the same—Christ our Blessed Lord, and the ends for which

the Sacrifice of the Mass is offered are the same as those of the sacrifice of the cross.

283. **What are the ends for which the sacrifice of the cross was offered?**
The ends for which the sacrifice of the cross was offered are: first, to honor and glorify God; second, to thank him for all the graces bestowed on the whole world; third, to satisfy God's justice for the sins of men; fourth, to obtain all graces and blessings.

284. **What is the difference between the sacrifice of the cross and the Sacrifice of the Mass?**
The only difference between the two sacrifices is that, on the cross, Jesus Christ offered himself by really shedding his blood; whereas, on the altar, he is offered by the priest without shedding his blood, nor dying.

285. **How does the Mass represent the death of Jesus Christ?**
The Mass represents the death of Jesus Christ by the separate consecration of the bread and of the wine.

* 286. **How should we assist at Mass?**
We should assist at Mass with great interior recollection and piety and with every outward mark of respect and devotion.

287. **Which is the best manner of hearing Mass?**
The best manner of hearing Mass is to offer it to God with the priest for the same purpose for which it is said, to meditate on Christ's sufferings, and to go to Communion.

288. **To whom do we offer the Sacrifice of the Mass?**
We offer the Sacrifice of the Mass to God only, because the sacrifice is an act of adoration which is due to God alone.

On Extreme Unction and Holy Orders

289. **What is extreme unction?**

Extreme unction is the sacrament which, through the anointing and prayers of the priest, gives health and strength to the soul, and sometimes to the body, when we are in danger of death from sickness.

290. **When should we receive extreme unction?**

We should receive extreme unction when we are in danger of death from sickness, or from a wound or accident.

291. **Should we wait until we are in extreme danger before we receive extreme unction?**

No, we should not wait until we are in extreme danger before we receive extreme unction, but, if possible, we should receive it whilst we have the use of our senses, so as to receive it with greater benefit to our soul, and not to expose ourselves to be deprived of this sacrament.

* 292. **Which are the effects of the sacrament of extreme unction?**

The effects of the sacrament of extreme unction are: 1) to comfort us in the pains of sickness and to strengthen us against temptation; 2) to remit venial sins and to cleanse our souls from the remains of sin; 3) to restore us to health when God sees fit.

293. **What do you mean by "the remains of sin"?**

By "the remains of sin," I mean 1) the punishment due to sin; 2) the inclination to evil and the weakness of the will which are the result of our sins, and which remain after our sins have been forgiven.

* 294. **How should we receive the sacrament of extreme unction?**

We should receive the sacrament of extreme unction in the state of grace, and with lively faith and resignation to the will of God.

295. **Who are the ministers of extreme unction?**
Bishops and priests are the ministers of extreme unction.

* 296. **What is holy orders?**
Holy orders is a sacrament which gives to bishops, priests, and other ministers of the Church power and grace to perform their ecclesiastical duties.

297. **What is necessary to receive holy orders worthily?**
To receive holy orders worthily, it is necessary to have a divine call to this sacred office, to have the necessary knowledge, and to be in a state of grace.

298. **How should Christians look upon the priests of the Church?**
Christians should look upon the priests of the Church as the messengers of God and the dispensers of his doctrine and of his graces.

299. **Who can confer the sacrament of holy orders?**
Only bishops can confer the sacrament of holy orders.

On Matrimony

* 300. **What is the sacrament of matrimony?**
Matrimony is the sacrament which unites a Christian man and woman in lawful marriage and gives them grace to live in a Christian manner.

301. **Can a Christian man and woman be united in lawful marriage in any other way than by the sacrament of matrimony?**
No, a Christian man and woman cannot be united in lawful marriage in any other way than by the sacrament of matrimony, because Jesus Christ raised marriage to the dignity of a sacrament.

302. **What should we think of persons who are married only by civil law?**
Persons who are married only by civil law are in a state of habitual mortal sin, and their union is not legitimate before God, because it is not formed according to the laws of the Church.

303. **Can the bond of Christian marriage be dissolved by any human power?**
No, the bond of Christian marriage cannot be dissolved by any human power; this bond can be broken only by the death of the husband or wife.

* 304. **Which are the effects of the sacrament of matrimony?**
The effects of the sacrament of matrimony are: 1) to sanctify the love of husband and wife; 2) to give them grace to bear each other's weaknesses; 3) to enable them to bring up their children in the fear and love of God.

* 305. **What is necessary to receive worthily the sacrament of matrimony?**
To receive worthily the sacrament of matrimony, it is necessary to be in a state of grace, and to comply with the laws of the Church.

306. **Who has the right to make laws concerning the sacrament of marriage?**
The Church alone has the right to make laws concerning the sacrament of marriage, though the state also has the power to make laws concerning the civil effects of marriage.

307. **Why does the Church forbid the marriage of Catholics with persons who have a different religion or no religion at all?**
The Church forbids the marriage of Catholics with persons who have a different religion or no religion at all, because such marriages generally lead to indifference with regard to religion, to loss of faith, and to the neglect of the religious education of the children.

308. **Why do many marriages prove unhappy?**
Many marriages prove unhappy because they are entered into without reflection, or from motives unworthy of a Christian.

309. **How should Christians prepare for a holy and happy marriage?**
Christians should prepare for a holy and happy marriage by receiving the sacraments of penance and Holy Eucharist; by begging God to grant them a pure intention and to direct their choice; and by asking the advice of their parents and the blessing of their pastor.

310. **In whose presence should marriage be contracted?**
Marriage should be contracted in presence of the pastor; and before two witnesses, at least.

311. **What do you mean by "marriage being forbidden between relatives within the fourth degree of kindred"?**
By "marriage being forbidden between relatives as far as the fourth degree inclusively," I mean that a marriage contracted by relatives within this degree is not valid, unless a dispensation has been obtained which ecclesiastical authority grants for sufficient reasons only.

312. **What is meant by the command "not to solemnize marriage at forbidden times"?**
The command "not to solemnize marriage at forbidden times" means that, during Advent and Lent, marriage cannot be accompanied with pomp nor a nuptial Mass.

313. **What is a nuptial Mass?**
It is a Mass at which the priest, in the name of the Church, prays in a special manner for the contracting couple, and gives them a special benediction.

On the Sacramentals

* 314. **What are sacramentals?**

Sacramentals are things set apart or blessed by the Church to excite good thoughts and to increase devotion, and thereby to obtain for us the remission of our venial sins.

315. **What is the difference between the sacraments and the sacramentals?**

The difference between the sacraments and the sacramentals is twofold: 1) the sacraments were instituted by Jesus Christ; whereas the sacramentals were instituted by the Church; 2) the sacraments give grace of themselves, provided we place no obstacle in the way; whereas the sacramentals merely incite in us pious dispositions by means of which we may obtain grace.

* 316. **Which is the chief of the sacramentals and the one most in use?**

The chief of the sacramentals and the one most in use is the sign of the cross.

* 317. **How do we make the sign of the cross?**

We make the sign of the cross by putting the right hand to the forehead, then to the breast, and then to the left and right shoulders, saying: "In the name of the Father, and of the Son, and of the Holy Ghost. Amen."

* 318. **Why do we make the sign of the cross?**

We make the sign of the cross to show that we are Christians, and that we believe the principal mysteries of our religion.

319. **How is the sign of the cross a profession of faith in the principal mysteries of our religion?**

The sign of the cross is a profession of faith in the principal mysteries of our religion because it expresses the mysteries of one God in three Persons, of the incarnation, and of the redemption.

320. **How does the sign of the cross express the mystery of one God in three Persons?**
The words "in the name" express the mystery of one God; the words that follow, "of the Father, and of the Son, and of the Holy Ghost," express the three divine Persons.

321. **How does the sign of the cross express the mysteries of the incarnation and of the redemption?**
The sign of the cross expresses the mysteries of the incarnation and of the redemption by reminding us that the Son of God, having become man, suffered death on the cross to redeem us.

* 322. **After the sign of the cross, which sacramental is in most frequent use?**
After the sign of the cross, the sacramental in most frequent use is holy water.

* 323. **What is holy water?**
Holy water is water blessed by the priest with solemn prayer to beg God's blessing on those who use it, and protection from the powers of hell.

324. **Are there any other sacramentals besides the sign of the cross and holy water?**
Yes; besides the sign of the cross and holy water there are many sacramentals, such as blessed candles, palms, crucifixes, images, rosaries, scapulars...

On Prayer

On Prayer in General

* 325. **What is prayer?**

Prayer is the lifting up of our minds and hearts to God to adore him, to thank him for his benefits, to ask his forgiveness, or to beg of him the graces we need for soul or body.

* 326. **Is prayer necessary to salvation?**

Yes, prayer is necessary to salvation, because, without it, no one having the use of reason can obtain the graces necessary to avoid evil and to do good.

* 327. **When must we pray?**

We must often pray, but particularly on Sundays and holy days; every day, both morning and night; and in all dangers, temptations, and afflictions.

328. **How should we pray?**

We should pray 1) with attention; 2) with humility, by acknowledging our own helplessness and dependence upon God; 3) with great confidence in God and a great desire to obtain his graces; 4) with perseverance.

329. **In whose name must we pray?**

We must pray in the name of our Lord Jesus Christ, who has promised us that his Father will grant whatsoever we ask in his name.

330. **For whom should we pray?**

We should pray for everyone without exception, and particularly for all those who have authority over us, for our benefactors, for our enemies, for sinners, and the faithful departed.

331. **Does God always hear our prayers?**

Yes, God always hears our prayers when they are well said; but he grants our requests in the way he knows to be most useful for our salvation.

332. **What above all should we ask of God?**

We should ask God above all for those things which concern his glory, our own and our neighbor's salvation.

333. **May we ask God for health and for other temporal blessings?**

Yes, we may ask God for health and other temporal blessings, provided we do so with submission to his will.

* 334. **Which are the prayers most recommended to us?**

The prayers most recommended to us are the Lord's Prayer, the Hail Mary, the Apostles' Creed, the *confiteor*, and the acts of faith, hope, love, and contrition.

On the Lord's Prayer

335. **Who taught us the Our Father or Lord's Prayer?**

It is Jesus Christ himself who taught us the Our Father or Lord's Prayer.

* 336. **Recite the Lord's Prayer.**

Our Father who art in heaven.

1. Hallowed be thy name.
2. Thy kingdom come.
3. Thy will be done on earth as it is in heaven.
4. Give us this day our daily bread.
5. And forgive us our trespasses, as we forgive them who trespass against us.
6. And lead us not into temptation.
7. But deliver us from evil. Amen.

* 337. **Why do you say, "Our Father," and not, "My Father"?**
We say, "Our Father," and not, "My Father," because God is the Creator or Father of all men, and consequently we are all children of a same family.

338. **Why did our Lord add, "who art in heaven"?**
Our Lord added, "who art in heaven," to teach us to lift our hearts to heaven where God reigns in his glory and where we hope to possess him one day.

* 339. **What do we ask of God in the Lord's Prayer?**
In the Lord's Prayer, we ask of God all that may contribute to his glory, and all that is necessary for the life of soul and body.

340. **What do we ask for the glory of God?**
We ask three things for the glory of God: 1) that his holy name be known and blessed; 2) that he may reign in all hearts by his grace; 3) that all creatures obey him on earth, as the angels and saints obey him in heaven.

341. **What do we ask for ourselves in the Lord's Prayer?**
In the Lord's Prayer, we ask four things for ourselves: 1) our daily bread, that is to say, spiritual and temporal goods; 2) the forgiveness of our sins, remembering that we must forgive our neighbor if we wish God to forgive us; 3) the grace of overcoming temptation; 4) the favor of being preserved from all evil, particularly from sin and eternal damnation.

342. **What is expressed by the word *Amen* or "So be it"?**
The word *Amen* or "So be it" expresses a more ardent desire to obtain what we ask, and it is for this reason that it is placed at the end of nearly every prayer.

On the Angelical Salutation

* 343. **Why do we so often pray to the Blessed Virgin?**
We pray often to the Blessed Virgin because she is the most powerful protectress we can have in heaven.

344. **By what prayer does the Church most usually invoke the Blessed Virgin?**
It is by the Hail Mary, also called the "Angelical Salutation," that the Church most usually invokes the Blessed Virgin.

* 345. **Recite the Angelical Salutation.**
Hail Mary, full of grace, the Lord is with thee; blessed art thou amongst women, and blessed is the fruit of thy womb, Jesus.

Holy Mary, Mother of God, pray for us sinners, now and at the hour of our death. Amen.

346. **Why do we call this prayer the "Angelical Salutation"?**
We call this prayer the "Angelical Salutation," because it begins with the words by which the angel Gabriel saluted the Blessed Virgin, in announcing to her that she would become Mother of God.[10]

347. **What is the meaning of these words, "full of grace," which the angel addressed to Mary?**
These words mean that the Blessed Virgin Mary, by a special privilege, and through the merits of Jesus Christ, was preserved from the stain of original sin, and filled with grace from the first moment of her existence.

348. **What is the meaning of these words of the angel to Mary: "The Lord is with thee"?**
These words of the angel to Mary mean that she is united to God in the most intimate manner and is about to become a living temple in which the incarnate Word will corporally dwell.

[10] Cf. Lk 1:28

349. **What is the meaning of these words of St. Elizabeth to the Blessed Virgin: "Blessed art thou amongst women"?**[11]
These words mean that Mary is superior to all women, not only on account of her immaculate conception, but, above all, on account of her incomparable dignity of Mother of God.

350. **What is the meaning of these other words of St. Elizabeth to Mary: "And blessed is the fruit of thy womb, Jesus"?**[12]
These words mean that the Son of Mary is holiness itself, and that we should rejoice with her, because he is glorified by his Father and adored by man.

351. **What do we acknowledge by this prayer of the Church: "Holy Mary, Mother of God, pray for us sinners, now and at the hour of our death. Amen"?**
By this prayer, we acknowledge Mary to be holy and the Mother of God; and full of confidence in her power, we implore her to obtain for us by her prayers to live and die, as she did, in a holy manner, in order, one day, to be associated with her in heaven.

* 352. **What sentiments should we cherish for the Blessed Virgin?**
For the Blessed Virgin, we should cherish sentiments of profound respect, tender love, firm and unlimited confidence, because she is the Mother of God and our Mother also.

353. **Is the Blessed Virgin truly the Mother of God?**
Yes, the Blessed Virgin is truly the Mother of God, because the same Person who is the Son of God is also the Son of the Blessed Virgin Mary.

[11] Lk 1:42
[12] Ibid.

354. **How can we say that the Mother of Jesus Christ is also our Mother?**
We can say that Mary is our Mother, because Jesus Christ, on the cross, wished his Mother to adopt us, in the person of Saint John, as her children, when he said to Mary: "Behold thy Son";[13] and to Saint John: "Behold thy Mother."[14]

* 355. **What should we do to show our devotion for the Blessed Virgin?**
To show our devotion to the Blessed Virgin, we should frequently invoke her, celebrate her feasts with piety, and strive to imitate her virtues.

356. **What pious ways of paying honor to the Blessed Virgin has the Church authorized?**
The Church has authorized several pious ways of paying honor to the Blessed Virgin: such are the beads, the rosary, the *Angelus*, sodalities, confraternities of the scapulars of Our Lady of Mount Carmel, and of the Immaculate Conception, etc.

On the Commandments of God

* 357. **Is it sufficient to belong to the Church of God to be saved?**
No, it is not sufficient to belong to the Church of God to be saved; we must moreover observe the commandments of God and of the Church.

* 358. **Which are the commandments that contain the whole law of God?**
The commandments that contain the whole law of God are the following two: 1) Thou shalt love the Lord thy God with thy whole heart, with thy whole soul, with thy whole strength, and with thy whole mind. 2) Thou shalt love thy neighbor as thyself, for the love of God.

[13] Jn 19:26
[14] Jn 19:27

359. **Why do you say that these two commandments of the love of God and of our neighbor contain the whole law of God?**
I say that these two commandments of the love of God and of our neighbor contain the whole law of God, because all the other commandments have been given to us but to enable us to know and to observe these two commandments.

* 360. **Recite the abridgment of the commandments of God.**

1. I am the Lord thy God, thou shalt not have strange gods before me.
2. Thou shalt not take the name of the Lord thy God in vain.
3. Remember that thou keep holy the sabbath day.
4. Honor thy father and thy mother.
5. Thou shalt not kill.
6. Thou shalt not commit adultery.
7. Thou shalt not steal.
8. Thou shalt not bear false witness against thy neighbor.
9. Thou shalt not covet thy neighbor's wife.
10. Thou shalt not covet thy neighbor's goods.

361. **Who gave the ten commandments?**
God himself, who gave them to Moses, on Mount Sinai, and Jesus Christ confirmed them in his gospel.

On the First Commandment of God

* 362. **Which is the first commandment of God?**
The first commandment of God is: "I am the Lord thy God,...thou shalt not have strange gods before me."[15]

[15] Ex 20:2-3

363. **How does the first commandment help us to keep the great commandment of the love of God?**
The first commandment helps us to keep the great commandment of the love of God, because it commands us to adore God alone.

* 364. **How do we adore God?**
We adore God by faith, hope, and charity; and by the worship we give him as Creator and sovereign master of all things.

* 365. **How do we break the first commandment of God?**
We break the first commandment of God: 1) by giving to any creature the honor which belongs to God alone; 2) by giving false worship to God; 3) by attributing to any creature a perfection which belongs to God alone.

366. **Is it allowed to make use of spells and charms, to credit dreams, spiritists, and fortune tellers?**
No; it is not allowed, because by so doing we attribute to creatures perfections and power which belong to God alone.

* 367. **Do we sin against the first commandment of God when we sin against faith, hope, and charity?**
Yes, we sin against the first commandment of God when we sin against faith, hope, and charity.

* 368. **How do we sin against faith?**
We sin against faith: 1) when we willfully doubt any revealed truth; 2) when we refuse to believe what God teaches us by his Church; 3) when we are ashamed to pass for a Christian or when we formally deny our faith; 4) when we neglect to learn sufficiently the Christian doctrine.

369. **Who are they who refuse to believe what God teaches by his Church?**
Heretics and infidels are they who refuse to believe what God teaches by his Church.

370. **Is it a great fault not to openly profess our faith in the true Church in which we inwardly believe?**

Yes, it is a great fault not to openly profess our faith in the true Church when we inwardly believe in it, because our Lord has said: "Whosoever shall deny me before men, I will also deny him before my Father who is in heaven."[16]

* 371. **Are we often obliged to make open profession of our faith?**

Yes we are obliged to make open profession of our faith as often as God's honor, our neighbor's spiritual good, or our own requires it: "Whosoever," says Christ, "shall confess me before men, I will also confess him before my Father who is in heaven."[17]

* 372. **Which are the sins against hope?**

The sins against hope are presumption and despair.

* 373. **What is presumption?**

Presumption is a rash expectation of salvation through which we rely on God's mercy as a license to commit sin and to delay our conversion.

* 374. **What is despair?**

Despair is the loss of hope in God's mercy regarding our conversion and eternal salvation.

375. **How do we sin against the love of God?**

We sin against the love of God by all sin, but particularly by mortal sin.

[16] Mt 10:33
[17] Mt 10:32

The First Commandment: On the Worship and Invocation of Saints

* 376. **Does the first commandment forbid the honoring of the saints?**

No, the first commandment does not forbid the honoring of the saints; on the contrary, it rather approves of this worship, because by honoring the saints, who are the chosen friends of God, we honor God himself.

* 377. **Does the first commandment forbid us to invoke the saints by asking their help and intercession?**

No, the first commandment does not forbid us to invoke the saints by asking their help and intercession.

378. **How do we know that the saints hear us?**

We know that the saints hear us because they are with God, who makes our prayers known to them.

379. **Why do we believe that the saints will help us?**

We believe that the saints will help us because we are brethren and members of the same Church, and because of the miracles obtained by their intercession.

380. **How are the saints and we members of the same Church?**

The saints and we are members of the same Church because the bonds of charity, which united them during life to the Church militant, are not broken by their entrance into the Church triumphant.

381. **What is the communion of saints?**

The communion of saints signifies the mutual union which charity establishes between the living members of the Church, the blessed in heaven, and the souls suffering in purgatory.

382. **What benefits result from the communion of saints?**
Two benefits result from the communion of saints: 1) the faithful on earth assist one another by their prayers and good works, and they are aided by the intercession of the saints in heaven; 2) the souls in purgatory are relieved by the saints in heaven and the faithful on earth.

383. **What do you understand by "the relics of the saints"?**
By "the relics of the saints," I understand all that remains of their bodies and the objects directly connected with them.

384. **Does the first commandment forbid us to honor the relics of the saints?**
No, the first commandment does not forbid us to honor the relics of the saints, because this honor refers to God, whose friends the saints are.

* 385. **Does the first commandment forbid the making of images?**
The first commandment does forbid the making of images if they are made to be adored as gods; but it does not forbid the making of them to put us in mind of Jesus Christ, his Blessed Mother, and the saints.

386. **Is it right to show respect to the images of Jesus Christ and the saints?**
Yes, it is right to show respect to the images of Jesus Christ and the saints, because they represent Jesus Christ and the saints.

387. **Is it allowed to pray to the crucifix or to the images and relics of the saints?**
No, it is not allowed to pray to the crucifix, or to the images and relics of the saints, for they have no life nor power nor faculty to help or hear us.

* 388. **Why do we pray before the crucifix, images, and the relics of the saints?**
We pray before the crucifix and the images and relics of the saints, because these objects excite our devotion, by reminding us of Jesus Christ and his saints, that we may imitate their virtues.

On the Second and Third Commandments of God

On the Second Commandment of God

* 389. **What is the second commandment of God?**

The second commandment of God is: "Thou shalt not take the name of the Lord thy God in vain."[18]

* 390. **What are we commanded by the second commandment?**

We are commanded by the second commandment to speak with reverence of God, and of the saints and of holy things; and to keep our lawful oaths and vows.

* 391. **What is an oath?**

An oath is to take God as witness of the truth of what we say.

392. **When may we take an oath?**

We may take an oath in serious circumstances, as when we are compelled to do so by lawful authority, or when it is necessary for God's honor, or for our own or our neighbor's good.

393. **What is swearing in vain?**

Swearing in vain is: 1) to take an oath without necessity; 2) to affirm on oath what we know to be false—this is called perjury; 3) to bind one's self by oath to do something forbidden.

394. **Is perjury, or a false oath, a great sin?**

Perjury, or a false oath, is in itself a mortal sin, because it is a serious injury to God by seeming to make him partaker in the lie.

[18] Ex 20:7

395. **He who has sworn to do an unlawful act, is he obliged to keep his oath?**
No, he who has sworn to do an unlawful act is not obliged to keep his oath; because he was guilty of a fault in taking the oath, and he would be guilty of another in keeping it.

* 396. **What is a vow?**
A vow is a deliberate promise made to God with the intention of binding ourselves rigorously to accomplish something which is agreeable to him.

* 397. **Is it a sin not to keep our vows?**
Yes, it is a sin not to keep our vows, and this sin is mortal or venial according to the nature of the vow and the intention we had in taking it.

398. **Is it right to make vows?**
Yes, it is right to make vows, since it is an excellent means of honoring God; however it is prudent never to make them without mature reflection, nor without the advice of one's confessor.

* 399. **What is forbidden by the second commandment?**
The second commandment forbids all false, rash, unjust, and unnecessary swearing, as well as blasphemy and cursing.

* 400. **What is blasphemy?**
Blasphemy is the use of injurious words against God or the saints, and above all to profane the holy name of God.

* 401. **Is blasphemy a great sin?**
Yes, blasphemy is a great sin, which God often punishes even in this world.

On the Third Commandment of God

* 402. **What is the third commandment of God?**
The third commandment is: "Remember that thou keep holy the sabbath day."[19]

* 403. **What is commanded by the third commandment?**
By the third commandment, we are commanded to sanctify the Sunday which is called the Lord's day, because this day should be specially employed in the service and worship of God.

404. **Are the sabbath day and the Sunday the same?**
No, because the sabbath sanctified by the Jews was the seventh day of the week, but Sunday which is sanctified by Christians is the first day of the week.

405. **Why does the Church command us to keep the Sunday holy instead of the sabbath?**
The Church commands us to sanctify the Sunday, because on that day our Lord rose from the dead, and on Sunday he sent the Holy Ghost upon the apostles.

* 406. **How are we to honor God on Sunday?**
We should honor God on Sundays by assisting at Holy Mass; and by abstaining from servile works which are not necessary.

407. **What sin does a person commit who does not assist at Mass on Sunday when he can do so?**
A person who does not assist at Mass on Sunday when he can do so commits a mortal sin.

408. **What do you mean by "servile works"?**
Servile works are those which require labor rather of the body than of the mind.

[19] Ex 20:8

* 409. **Are servile works on Sunday ever lawful?**
Servile works are lawful on Sunday when the glory of God, charity due to our neighbor, or necessity requires them.

On the Fourth, Fifth, and Sixth Commandments of God

On the Fourth Commandment of God

* 410. **What is the fourth commandment of God?**
The fourth commandment is: "Honor thy father and thy mother."[20]

* 411. **How should we honor our parents?**
We should honor our parents by loving them, by respecting them, by assisting them, and by obeying them in all that is not sin.

* 412. **Why should we love our father and our mother?**
We should love our father and our mother, because after God it is to them we owe our life, and because he has charged them to provide for our chief wants.

413. **How do we respect our father and mother?**
We respect our father and mother by treating them with deference, bearing patiently with their infirmities, and even with their defects.

* 414. **Why should we respect our father and mother?**
We should respect our father and mother because they hold God's place over us.

[20] Ex 20:12

* 415. **Why should we obey our father and mother?**
We should obey our father and mother because in obeying them it is God we obey.

416. **Why should we assist our father and mother?**
We should assist our father and mother because it is very just that we render to them in their wants all that we have ourselves received from them.

417. **How should we assist our father and mother?**
We should assist our father and mother by procuring for them, as far as we can, all spiritual and temporal help in time of malady, in old age, and in poverty, and by praying for them after their death.

* 418. **What is the meaning of these words: "That thou mayest be longlived"?**[21]
These words signify that God often rewards, even in this life, the child who honors his father and mother.

* 419. **What punishment is inflicted upon children who outrage their father and mother, or who abandon them in their necessities?**
Children who outrage their father and mother, or who abandon them in their necessities, are cursed by God, and are held in execration by man.

* 420. **Are our father and mother the only persons to whom we owe honor and obedience?**
No, for we should honor and obey all those who have authority over us, such as bishops, pastors, magistrates, masters, and lawful superiors.

421. **What are the duties of fathers and mothers toward their children?**
Fathers and mothers are obliged to provide for the wants of their children, to bring them up in a Christian manner, to correct their defects, to keep them from all spiritual and corporal danger, and to give them good example.

[21] Ibid.

422. **What are the duties of superiors toward inferiors?**
Superiors should treat their inferiors with charity, watch over their conduct, and facilitate for them the means to accomplish their duties of religion.

423. **What are the duties of inferiors toward superiors?**
The duties of inferiors toward superiors are to respect and to obey them.

* 424. **What is forbidden by the fourth commandment?**
The fourth commandment forbids all disobedience, stubbornness, and contempt toward father, mother, or superiors.

On the Fifth Commandment of God

* 425. **What is the fifth commandment of God?**
The fifth commandment of God is: "Thou shall not kill."[22]

* 426. **What is commanded by the fifth commandment?**
By the fifth commandment, we are commanded to respect our own and our neighbor's spiritual and corporal life.

* 427. **What is forbidden by the fifth commandment?**
The fifth commandment forbids us: 1) to take away our own life or the life of others, or even to desire to do so; 2) to wound or to strike or to hate our neighbor; to say injurious words and to revenge; 3) to give scandal.

* 428. **What do you mean by "scandalizing our neighbor"?**
By "scandalizing our neighbor," I mean to lead him into evil by bad advice or bad example, and thus expose ourselves to give death to his soul.

[22] Ex 20:13

* 429. **Are we obliged to repair the evil we have done our neighbor?**
Yes, we are obliged to repair the evil we have done our neighbor by scandal, by detraction or by calumny, by injury or by bad treatment.

On the Sixth Commandment of God

* 430. **What is the sixth commandment of God?**
The sixth commandment of God is: "Thou shalt not commit adultery."[23]

* 431. **What is commanded by the sixth commandment?**
We are commanded by the sixth commandment to be pure in thought, and modest in all our thoughts, words, and actions.

* 432. **What is forbidden by the sixth commandment?**
The sixth commandment forbids: 1) all unchaste freedom with another's wife or husband; 2) all immodesty with ourselves or others in look, word, or action; 3) all immodesty in dress; 4) everything that leads to impurity, such as immodest pictures and shows, fast dances, immoral books and newspapers.

On the Seventh, Eighth, Ninth, and Tenth Commandments of God

On the Seventh Commandment of God

* 433. **Which is the seventh commandment of God?**
The seventh commandment of God is: "Thou shalt not steal."[24]

[23] Ex 20:14
[24] Ex 20:15

* 434. **What is commanded by the seventh commandment?**
By the seventh commandment, we are commanded to give everyone what belongs to him, and to respect his property.

* 435. **What is forbidden by the seventh commandment?**
The seventh commandment forbids all unjust taking or keeping what belongs to our neighbor, or doing him any injustice.

436. **Who are they who take unjustly what belongs to another?**
They who take unjustly what belongs to another are robbers, unfaithful servants, dishonest merchants, usurers, dishonest litigants, and generally all those who wrong their neighbor.

* 437. **Are we bound to restore ill-gotten goods?**
Yes, we are bound to restore ill-gotten goods, or the value of them, as far as we are able, otherwise we cannot obtain pardon of our sins, nor be saved.

* 438. **Are we obliged to repair the damage we have unjustly caused?**
Yes, we are obliged to repair the damage we have unjustly caused.

439. **How do we unjustly retain what belongs to another?**
We unjustly retain what belongs to another by not paying our debts when we can do so, by not restoring an object confided to us, or by keeping anything we find without seeking the rightful owner.

On the Eighth Commandment of God

* 440. **What is the eighth commandment of God?**
The eighth commandment of God is: "Thou shalt not bear false witness against thy neighbor."[25]

[25] Ex 20:16

* 441. **What are we commanded by the eighth commandment?**
By the eighth commandment, we are commanded to speak the truth in all things, and to respect our neighbor's honor and reputation.

* 442. **What is forbidden by the eighth commandment?**
The eighth commandment forbids false testimony, detraction, calumny, and lies.

443. **What is false testimony?**
False testimony is an evidence, contrary to truth, given before a tribunal.

444. **What is a rash judgment?**
A rash judgment is a bad opinion of our neighbor, formed without sufficient proofs.

445. **What is detraction?**
Detraction is making known, without necessity, the real faults or defects of our neighbor.

446. **How can we repair the evil done our neighbor by detraction?**
We can repair the evil done our neighbor by detraction, by excusing his faults and by praising his good qualities.

447. **What is calumny?**
Calumny is a false accusation against our neighbor by which we attribute to him a defect which he does not possess, or accuse him of a fault which he has not committed.

448. **How should we repair the evil done our neighbor by calumny?**
We should repair the evil done our neighbor by calumny, by retracting the falsehood spoken against him.

On the Ninth Commandment of God

* 449. **What is the ninth commandment of God?**
The ninth commandment of God is: "Thou shalt not covet thy neighbor's wife."[26]

* 450. **What is commanded by the ninth commandment?**
We are commanded by the ninth commandment to keep ourselves pure in thought and desire.

* 451. **What is forbidden by the ninth commandment?**
The ninth commandment forbids: 1) all unchaste thoughts and desires of another's wife or husband; 2) all other carnal thoughts and desires.

* 452. **Are impure thoughts and desires always sins?**
Impure thoughts and desires are always mortal sins, if we consent to them.

* 453. **Which are the means to be employed to avoid these sins?**
The means to be employed to avoid these sins are the avoidance of all dangerous occasions, prayer, the frequent reception of the sacraments, and devotion to the Blessed Virgin.

On the Tenth Commandment of God

* 454. **What is the tenth commandment of God?**
The tenth commandment of God is: "Thou shalt not covet thy neighbor's goods."[27]

[26] Ex 20:17
[27] Ibid.

* 455. **What are we commanded by the tenth commandment?**
We are commanded by the tenth commandment to rejoice in our neighbor's welfare, and to repress the desire to take or to keep unjustly what belongs to another.

On the First and Second Commandments of the Church

* 456. **Which are the principal commandments of the Church?**

1. Thou shalt sanctify the holy days which are commanded thee.
2. Thou shalt hear Mass on Sundays and holy days.
3. Thou shalt confess thy sins at least once a year.
4. Thou shalt humbly receive thy Creator, at least at Easter time.
5. Thou shalt fast on the Ember days, vigils, and throughout Lent.
6. Thou shalt not eat flesh meat on Fridays or Saturdays.
7. Thou shalt faithfully pay to the Church her rights and tithes.

* 457. **Are we obliged to observe the commandments of the Church?**
Yes, we are strictly obliged to observe the commandments of the Church, because it is Jesus Christ himself who has given the Church power to make these laws, and he wishes us to obey them.

On the First Commandment of the Church

* 458. **What is commanded by the first commandment: "Thou shalt sanctify the holy days which are commanded thee"?**
We are commanded by the first commandment to sanctify the holy days of obligation designated by the Church.

459. **Why were holy days instituted by the Church?**
Holy days were instituted by the Church to recall to our minds the great mysteries of religion and the virtues and glory of the saints.

460. **How should we keep holy days of obligation?**
We should keep holy days of obligation as we should keep the Sunday: by assisting at Mass and abstaining from servile works.

On the Second Commandment of the Church

* 461. **What is commanded by the second commandment of the Church: "Thou shalt hear Mass on Sundays and holy days"?**
By the second commandment of the Church, we are commanded to assist at Mass on Sundays and holy days of obligation.

* 462. **How should we assist at Mass so as to fulfill the precept of the Church?**
To fulfill the precept of the Church, we must hear the entire Mass, with devotion, respect, and attention.

463. **Is it a mortal sin not to hear Mass on Sundays or holy days, or to prevent others from hearing it?**
Yes, it is a mortal sin 1) not to hear Mass on Sundays or holy days, without serious reasons; 2) to prevent, without sufficient reason, anyone from hearing Mass on the days commanded.

On the Third through the Seventh Commandments of the Church

On the Third Commandment of the Church

* 464. **What do you understand by the third commandment: "Thou shalt confess thy sins at least once a year"?**
By this commandment, I understand that we are all obliged to go to confession once a year, at least.

* 465. **To what are persons exposed who go but once a year to confession?**
Persons who go but once a year to confession deprive themselves of the graces of the sacrament, confirm themselves in their bad habits, and expose themselves to die in a state of sin.

* 466. **Are children obliged to go to confession?**
Yes, children are obliged to go to confession at the age of discretion, that is to say, when they sufficiently understand what it is to offend God mortally, which is commonly about the age of seven years.

On the Fourth Commandment of the Church

* 467. **What does the Church command us by the fourth commandment: "Thou shalt humbly receive thy Creator, at least at Easter time"?**
By this commandment, the Church commands all the faithful who have reached the age of discretion, to receive Holy Communion once a year, at least, and during the Easter time.

468. **What do you mean by "the age of discretion as regards Holy Communion"?**
"The age of discretion as regards Holy Communion" is when a child is sufficiently intelligent and instructed to receive this sacrament with the necessary dispositions.

469. **What sin does he commit who neglects to receive Communion during the Easter time?**
He who neglects to receive Communion during the Easter time commits a mortal sin, because he disobeys the Church in a grave matter, scorns the greatest favor of God, and scandalizes his neighbor.

470. **What is the Easter time?**
The Easter time, according to the general law of the Church, is the season which begins eight days before and ends eight days after Easter; but, in the province of Quebec, the pope allows it to begin on Ash Wednesday.

* 471. **Where should this Easter Communion be made?**
This Easter Communion should be made in our own parochial church; unless we have obtained permission from our pastor, or from our bishop to make it elsewhere.

On the Fifth Commandment of the Church

* 472. **What are we obliged to do by the fifth commandment of the Church: "Thou shalt fast on Ember days, vigils, and throughout Lent"?**
By this commandment, we are obliged to fast Wednesday, Friday, and Saturday of each of the Ember weeks; the Eve of Christmas, of Pentecost, of St. Peter, and St. Paul's day, of the Assumption, and of All Saints' day; as well as every Wednesday and Friday in Advent.

* 473. **What do you mean by "fast days"?**
By "fast days," I mean days on which we are allowed but one full meal, to which we may add a slight collation.

* 474. **What do you mean by "days of abstinence"?**
By "days of abstinence," I mean days on which we are forbidden to eat flesh meat, but are allowed the usual number of meals.

475. **Why does the Church command us to fast and abstain on certain days?**
The Church commands us to fast and abstain on certain days in order that we may mortify our passions and satisfy for our sins.

* 476. **At what age are we obliged to fast?**
The obligation of fasting begins the day we complete our twenty-first year.

477. **Which are the reasons that may exempt us from fasting?**
The reasons which may exempt us from fasting are a dispensation, illness, hard labor; in case of doubt, we should ask our confessor's advice.

On the Sixth Commandment of the Church

* 478. **What does the Church forbid by the sixth commandment: "Thou shalt not eat flesh meat on Fridays or Saturdays"?**
By the sixth commandment, the Church forbids us to use, without necessity, any flesh food on Friday and on Saturday. In this province, the sovereign pontiff has allowed the use of flesh food on Saturday when it is not a fast day.

* 479. **What is to be observed on the days of Lent on which, by dispensation, we are allowed to eat flesh meat?**
On the days in Lent on which, by dispensation, we are allowed to eat flesh meat, two conditions must be observed: 1) to eat but one flesh meal; 2) not to eat fish at this same meal.

480. **Which are the days in Lent on which, by dispensation, we are allowed to eat flesh meat?**
The days of Lent on which, by dispensation, we are allowed to eat flesh meat are: 1) every Sunday, except Palm Sunday; 2) every Monday, Tuesday, and Thursday, except the Thursday following Ash Wednesday and Holy Thursday.

481. **Why does the Church command us to abstain from meat on Fridays?**
The Church commands us to abstain from meat on Fridays to make us do penance on the day our Lord died for us.

On the Seventh Commandment of the Church

* 482. **What is commanded by the seventh commandment of the Church: "Thou shalt faithfully pay to the Church her rights and tithes"?**
We are commanded by this commandment to pay the tithes, supplements, poll-tax, and other dues authorized for the expenses of divine worship and for the support of the pastors.

On the Last Judgment and the Resurrection, Hell, Purgatory, and Heaven

* 483. **When will Jesus Christ judge us?**
Jesus Christ will first judge us immediately after our death, and again on the last day.

* 484. **What is the judgment called which we undergo immediately after our death?**
The judgment which we undergo immediately after our death is called "the particular judgment."

* 485. **What is the general judgment?**
The general judgment is that which all men have to undergo on the last day.

486. **Why does Jesus Christ judge men immediately after death?**
Jesus Christ judges men immediately after death to reward or punish them according to their deeds.

* 487. **Which are the rewards or punishments reserved for the souls of men after the particular judgment?**
The rewards or punishments reserved for the souls of men after the particular judgment are heaven, purgatory, and hell.

* 488. **What is hell?**
Hell is a place of torture for those who die in a state of mortal sin, in which they are deprived of the sight of God and suffer dreadful torments for all eternity.

* 489. **What is purgatory?**
Purgatory is a place of punishment in which suffer before going to heaven the souls of those who die guilty of venial sins, or without having satisfied for the temporal punishment due to their sins.

* 490. **Can the faithful on earth help the souls in purgatory?**
Yes, the faithful on earth can help the souls in purgatory by their prayers, their mortifications, their almsdeeds; by indulgences, by having Masses said, and by going to Communion for them.

491. **If everyone is judged immediately after death, what need is there of a general judgment?**
Though everyone is judged immediately after death, there is need of a general judgment, that God, who, on earth, often permits the good to suffer and the wicked to prosper, may in the end appear just before all men.

* 492. **Will our bodies share in the reward or punishment of our souls?**
Yes, our bodies will share in the reward or punishment of our souls, because, through the resurrection, they will be again united to them, to share their happiness or misery, as they had been sharers in their good deeds or in their sins.

493. **In what state will the bodies of the just rise?**
The bodies of the just will rise glorious and immortal.

494. **Will the bodies of the damned also rise?**
Yes the bodies of the damned will also rise, but they will be condemned to eternal punishment.

* 495. **What is heaven?**
Heaven is a place of bliss, in which the blessed see God face-to-face, participate in his glory, and enjoy eternal happiness.

*496. **Who are they who go to heaven?**
Those who go to heaven are the just who have never offended God, or who, having had the misfortune to offend him, have done penance.

497. **What words should we bear always in mind?**
We should bear always in mind these words of our Lord Jesus Christ: What doth it profit a man if he gain the whole world and suffer the loss of his own soul? Or what exchange shall a man give for his soul? For the Son of Man shall come in the glory of his Father with his angels; and then will he render to every man according to his works.[28]

[28] Cf. Mk 8:36-38; Rom 2:6

ABOUT THIS SERIES

Tradivox was first conceived as an international research endeavor to recover lost and otherwise little-known Catholic catechetical texts. As the research progressed over several years, the vision began to grow, along with the number of project contributors and a general desire to share these works with a broader audience.

Legally incorporated in 2019, Tradivox has begun the work of carefully remastering and republishing dozens of these catechisms which were once in common and official use in the Church around the world. That effort is embodied in this *Tradivox Catholic Catechism Index*, a multi-volume series restoring artifacts of traditional faith and praxis for a contemporary readership. More about this series and the work of Tradivox can be learned at www.Tradivox.com.

SOPHIA INSTITUTE

Sophia Institute is a nonprofit institution that seeks to nurture the spiritual, moral, and cultural life of souls and to spread the Gospel of Christ in conformity with the authentic teachings of the Roman Catholic Church.

Sophia Institute Press fulfills this mission by offering translations, reprints, and new publications that afford readers a rich source of the enduring wisdom of mankind.

Sophia Institute also operates the popular online resource CatholicExchange.com. *Catholic Exchange* provides world news from a Catholic perspective as well as daily devotionals and articles that will help readers to grow in holiness and live a life consistent with the teachings of the Church.

In 2013, Sophia Institute launched Sophia Institute for Teachers to renew and rebuild Catholic culture through service to Catholic education. With the goal of nurturing the spiritual, moral, and cultural life of souls, and an abiding respect for the role and work of teachers, we strive to provide materials and programs that are at once enlightening to the mind and ennobling to the heart; faithful and complete, as well as useful and practical.

Sophia Institute gratefully recognizes the Solidarity Association for preserving and encouraging the growth of our apostolate over the course of many years. Without their generous and timely support, this book would not be in your hands.

www.SophiaInstitute.com
www.CatholicExchange.com
www.SophiaInstituteforTeachers.org